THE HERO IN THE
FEMININE NOVEL

THE HERO
IN THE FEMININE NOVEL

GERARDA MARIA
KOOIMAN—VAN MIDDENDORP

HASKELL HOUSE
Publishers of Scholarly Books
NEW YORK
1966

published by

HASKELL HOUSE
Publishers of Scholarly Books
30 East 10th Street • New York, N. Y. 10003

PRINTED IN UNITED STATES OF AMERICA

CONTENTS

CHAPTER		PAGE
I.	THE HERO	1
II.	WOMAN AND WRITING	8
III.	APHRA BEHN	18
IV.	FRANCES BURNEY	24
V.	CLARA REEVE	31
VI.	ANN RADCLIFFE	35
VII.	ELIZABETH INCHBALD	39
VIII.	MARIA EDGEWORTH	43
IX.	JANE AUSTEN	49
X.	CHARLOTTE BRONTË	60
XI.	EMILY BRONTË	78
XII.	ELIZABETH CLEGHORN GASKELL	82
XIII.	GEORGE ELIOT	96
XIV.	MRS. HUMPHRY WARD	124
XV.	SUMMARY	153
	CONCLUSION	167
	BIBLIOGRAPHY	169

CHAPTER I.

THE HERO.

An author is a person, who looks deeper than most others into the hearts of people ; he sees through them, understands the motives of their actions, reveals secrets of which they are barely conscious themselves ; he is "celui qui a le plus senti la vie." [1] He feels a curious kind of love for his characters, even for the most repulsive ones ; he realizes their mental struggles, either leading to failure or success ; he views them all sub specie aeternitatis. With his own eyes he has seen them, with his own mind fathomed them and his inner life has projected itself in them.

Among the characters that he has created, there is one that is intended to appeal most to the mind of the reader ; the one that has come up from the depth of his soul, often the conveyor of the noblest thoughts and most heroic deeds, which his mind can imagine, the hero. Heroic characters are often exaggerated in order to set their virtues off the more distinctly as ideals by which to inspire common life. As an author is a child of his time, he will instinctively make his hero express the ideas of that time, the ways of thought, the 'mental atmosphere' dominant in the period, and the particular stage of development which the life of a nation has reached, for "the hero is he, who lives in the inward sphere of things.... ; he declares that abroad by act or speech." [2] At the same time his readers will become familiar with the author's own outlook on and conception of things ; they will

---

[1] J. J. Rousseau, *Emile*, Tome I, Livre I, p. 21.
[2] Th. Carlyle, *Hero and Heroworship*, Collins' Classics, Ch. V, p. 201.

get to know his character, as he cannot help revealing himself in the work he has written.

Now the conception of the hero is partly peculiar to the writer as an individual and partly dependent upon the society in which the writer moves, upon its ideals, aspirations and codes. The author's hero will tell us things about the author himself, but will likewise give information about his era. He sometimes has a presentiment of coming changes and preaches revolt against the prevailing ideas. A great writer is to be considered "the creator as well as the creature of his time." [1]) Louis Cazamian observes : "La psychologie du romancier, qui est moyen, nous donne prise sur le mouvement des consciences." [2])

The hero of the old romances was the living embodiment of what a childlike or ingenuous people dreamt he should be. He is the ideal knight devoted exclusively to glory and fame in war and joust. "They were comparatively picturesque and adventurous personages and men of action in the tented field.... In their characters of warriors and heroes they were men of mettle and had something in them." [3]) This hero is a conception firmly rooted in the mediaeval mind and is the hereditary type of all noble heroes for his mental qualities.

Lyly's Euphues is endowed with all the conceit and unreality of the Elizabethan period, but at the same time he manifests the interest the men of the Renaissance took in human life and character, the influence of the classical revival, the growth of national self-assertion and the consequent emancipation of the mind. "Dans l'idéal qu'il offre de l'homme cultivé, la recherche de l'élégance italienne ne cache point le sérieux moral de la Réforme." [4])

Nash in his *Unfortunate Traveller*, published in 1594, makes his hero, a cheerful, lighthearted and sharp-witted youth, pass through a succession of adventures and dangers, from which he

---
[1]) W. H. Hudson, *An Introduction to the Study of Literature*, p. 53.
[2]) L. Cazamian, *Le Roman Social en Angleterre*, Introduction, p. 15.
[3]) W. Hazlitt, *Essays and Sketches*, The World's Classics, p. 175/176.
[4]) L. Cazamian, *Le Roman Social en Angleterre*, Chap. III, p. 67.

narrowly escapes, whilst he has an opportunity of meeting all sorts of people, whom he satirizes. Jack Wilton is the ancestor of all the adventurous or picaresque heroes, embodying the spirit of adventure that exists, consciously or unconsciously, in every Englishman.

Christian in *The Pilgrim's Progress* by Bunyan [1] represents not only the struggles of the author's own soul through despair and temptations, by defeat and victory to final peace, but is at the same time the outcome of the religious unrest of the Puritan period.

Defoe, depicts in *Robinson Crusoe* not only the story of his own life, shipwrecked and ruined by party hatred, but also creates a hero, who is the pure representative of the national activity of his time. This hero is the ideal of the practical man, who by self-help and energetic efforts overcomes all his difficulties, or as Defoe himself says in the Introduction of his book: "while depicting a solitary individual struggling against misfortune, it indicates the justice and mercy of Providence and while inculcating the duty of self-help, asserts the complete dependence of man upon a higher power for all he stands in need of". In Robinsoe Crusoe the beginning of a tendency for reality is felt, which the then generation wanted.

Another novel, which reveals the spirit of adventure, is the work by which Swift lives in literature: his fascinating story of Gulliver, first a Surgeon and then a captain of ships, who has an opportunity of seeing many countries and nations and who compares them with his own. The author also uses his hero, however, to vent through him the hatred for mankind that

---

[1] Though some people will refuse to consider *The Pilgrim's Progress* as a novel, the reader's attention may be drawn to the opinion of Mr. G. Saintsbury given in *The English Novel* Ch. II p. 53 and 54: "It is impossible to share, and not very easy even to understand, the scruples of those who would not admit John Bunyan to a place in the hierarchy and the pedigree of the English novel, or would at best grant him an outside position in relation to it ...... Disregarding prejudice and punctilio everyone must surely see that, in diminishing measure, even *The Holy War* is a novel, and that *The Pilgrim's Progress* has everyone of the four requisites — plot, character, description and dialogue."

slumbers in his heart. The story of his adventures forms a fierce satire on humanity at large and was written to expose the results of civilisation in England.

Up till the 18th century a hero is always a rather bloodless figment; he and his deeds are taken from outside the common sphere. The rise of the middle-class, though not highly cultivated, brought with it a growing interest in life for life's sake, a longing for the concrete, a wish for a hero of flesh and blood, who is more in contact with reality. The greater sense of the importance of the inner feelings, and a conscious pleasure in one's own emotions, lead to the creation of the hero of sentimentality, who is endowed with all the good qualities, known to any living being. He is very rich, of high birth, has enjoyed a perfect education, is noble, generous, in short a picture of human perfection, the image of the ideal type at the bottom of his creator's heart. However, he is described with a didactic purpose and consequently becomes unreal. This hero, Sir Charles Grandison, English literature owes to Samuel Richardson. Together with the sentimental hero another instructive hero was born, but of a nature which suited the normal mind better. Fielding's Tom Jones is the realistic hero, who is "a philosophical unity, built up out of the experience itself of a human existence, out of the judgment of a gradually matured mind on the theatre in which it is at once a spectator and an actor." [1])

Idealize as they might, however, realistic authors required in any case an equal quantity of nature and truth in their heroes. Prince Rasselas was placed by Johnson in the world and was used to proclaim his didactic ideas of the natural life. The Vicar of Wakefield is a still more striking example of a hero moving about in the world.

A certain moral unrest, an increasing interest in the Middle Ages, a wish to see the present as a recurrence, a renewal of the past and a longing for the mysterious and the supernatural

---

[1]) Legouis and Cazamian, *A History of English Literature*, Vol. II, Bk. III, Ch. IV, p. 177.

awakens the imagination and finds its expression in the heroes of the romantic and historical school. To Walpole thanks are due for the happy blending of the supernatural and the realistic elements, and for characterisation by means of conversation in his description of the events which happen to the hero. In Sir Walter Scott culminates the romantic movement, when he produces Waverley, his hero of romance, as an actual human figure in historical surroundings.

Then the mind, however, gets more and more absorbed in practical considerations ; a rapid progress of science, the industrial revolution and owing to this an increase of democratic feelings, interest in education, in pauperism, in prisons and, last but not least, a growing interest in philosophic speculations lead to making the hero the conveyor of the author's interest in all these problems and to his revealing more and more "the thoughts and feelings, the aspirations and ideals, the doubts and struggles, the faith and hope of the period in which the creator lives." [1]

The hero, coloured by sentiment or romance or psychology, or conceived with a purpose of political or social reform, is no longer the perfect, faultless man of an imaginary world, no longer "the ideal hero, who believes nothing but what is true, feels nothing but what is exalted, and does nothing but what is graceful", because "the real heroes of God's making are quite different ; they have their natural heritage of love and conscience, which they draw in with their mother's milk ; they know one or two of those deep spiritual truths, which are only to be won by long wrestling with their own sins and their own sorrows ; they have earned faith and strength so far as they have done genuine work, but the rest is dry barren theory, blank prejudice, vague hearsay". [2] He will call forth sympathy, when we see in him 'a struggling, erring being like ourselves' and not when he is the mouthpiece of some author's thoughts or opinions or ideals. To produce an interest in a hero Hazlitt says: "There must be

---
[1] W. H. Hudson, *Introduction to the Study of Literature*, p. 49.
[2] G. Eliot, *Scenes of Clerical Life*, Collins' ed., p. 343.

mixed motives, alternate hope and fear, difficulties to struggle with, sacrifices to make". [1])

Now the question suggests itself : Is every hero a new product of imagination or reality ; is he a growth, an improvement on, a more perfect copy of, his predecessor ? It is self-evident that, in creating a character, a novelist will use not only the material that his observation of real life has enabled him to collect, but likewise hints, traits, views derived from the books he has read. Often enough the reading will have been an incitement to, or an aid in, observation of his own material. A new hero will be conceived with the original characteristics of some existing type altered by fusion with other characters. "Das Genie" says Dibelius in Kap. 12 of his *Englische Romankunst*, "arbeitet vielmehr oft mit ererbten literarischen typen ; es übernimmt Sie, weil Sie etwas unwesentliches sind, dasz des Autors Zwecke gestattet alle Kraft des groszen Problemen zuzuwenden, in denen er seine eigentliche Aufgabe erblickt. Für den Genius is der Typus ein hilfreicher Diener. Auch dem originellsten Geist dringt er sich auf um freilich abgeschüttelt oder originellen Beobachtung dienstbar gemacht zu werden". In an interesting article in the *Fortnightly Review*, Vol. XXIV, 1878, Professor Minto, who tried tro trace the origin of Mrs. Gaskell's novel *Mary Barton*, observes : "the vital principles are transmitted, and every plant in any cross section, that we may take of the stream of literary literature owes the fact that it lives at all to something which has lived before and has blossomed and born fruit and launched its fertilising seeds upon the great current." Tom Jones is already to be met in the picaresque hero ; he is Don Quixote in bourgeois surroundings, the mixture of good and bad qualities as Defoe pictured one in Robinson. Grandison is the continuation of the ideal courtier, who in his turn has his ancestors in the heroes of the romances of chivalry. Since the creation of heroes like Tom Jones and Grandison the types have become hereditary ;

---

[1]) W. Hazlitt, *Sketches and Essays*, World's Classics p. 175.

they have been repeated over and over again, albeit with modifications. The original types live on, for even in the types of realism the primitive elements of the ideals of fiction are found.

The present writer thought it interesting to consider the entent to which the lady-novelists have built on existing heroes, what they have made of them, and whether they have launched any new type into the world. Only one preliminary remark must be added ; as the chief person of a novel was originally a real hero, the name 'hero' was the right title for him. However, this word has gradually come to be used for the most prominent figure, even if this person did not perform any heroic deed at all, or perhaps played no part that called for a display of masculine character. Especially in such novels as have a female for the dominating character, the name 'hero' is rather objectionable. Yet for shortness' sake the old denomination, being more convenient, will be used in this discussion instead of 'principal male character'.

CHAPTER II.

WOMAN AND WRITING.

With the exception of Mrs. Aphra Behn, (the female pioneer in the field of prose-writing, who created a quite novel kind of hero and who had a host of imitators), women in England, with a few unimportant exceptions, did not attempt 'fiction' until the last quarter of the eighteenth century when the standard-types of heroes had already been evolved by male authors. There must be a cause which, in spite of Aphra Behn's example, prevented women from taking up writing, though the faculties necessary for it, are pre-eminently 'feminine', the chief of them being fantasy and quick observation.

Women have always been noted for the possession of fantasy, a gift, indeed, which may have been fostered by their seclusion from worldly affairs. What fantastic stories does not a woman tell about incidents of her life, which, in reality, are very insignificant, but are represented as if she were the heroine of some comedy or tragedy. Listen to the display of fantasy, when a woman tells a story to children. Have not women embroidered whole campaigns, lives of saints, formed in their minds of the stories they were told?

In power of observation women are certainly not behind men. When she is only a little girl a woman betrays her faculty of observation in the way in which she plays with her dolls. "Das Mädchen geht mit seiner Puppe wie mit einem Menschen um, es wiederholt mit ihr alle die Verhältnisse, die es um sich her beobachtet hat, es spricht und verkehrt mit ihr in ganz persönlicher Weise,"[1]) says Dr. Kluge. It is only a reproduction of

---

[1]) Dr. Med. Kluge, *Männliches und Weibliches Denken*, p. 14.

actions she has seen with her own eyes performed by grown-up persons round her and she makes her dolls act and speak in accurate imitation of those people. Professor Heymans observes: "Früheren Forscher sind im groszen und ganzen unter sich darüber einverstanden, dasz die Frauen besser wahrnehmen als die Männer." [1]) Laura Marholm calls the gift of keen observation "eine ganz weibliche Eigenschaft." [2]) Hazlitt expresses his opinion by saying: "women in general have a quicker perception of any singularity of character than men." [3])

Besides women are endowed with a specific female characteristic, Intuition, which, without conscious foundation, often gives good and valuable insight into persons and events. It is a kind of third eye, capable of understanding and looking into apparently impenetrable souls. It has also been compared to a kind of animal instinct. [4]) Hazlitt says that "this intuitive perception learns the idiom of character and manners by rote, without troubling itself about the principles." [5])

The fact that women did not take up novelwriting has, by some theorists, been attributed to mental inferiority. Others found the reason in circumstances in which they were situated, in the different education of men and women and in household demands.

The critic of the *Edinburgh Review* Dec. 1849 is of opinion that, "whereas a great work required 'the whole man' and that the best years for producing such a work are between twenty and forty, most women had to give their whole person to the cares and sufferings of Maternity." Ellen Key gives a similar

---

[1]) G. Heymans, *Die Psychologie der Frauen*, p. 85.
[2]) Laura Marholm, *Zur Psychologie der Frau*, p. 50.
[3]) W. Hazlitt, *Lectures on the English Comic Writers*, Collins' ed., p. 162.
[4]) A very good distinction between intuition and instinct is found in: Instinct is an unconscious knowledge; primitive man knows, but knows not why, cannot express consciously, that which speaks to him from within. In the intuition there is the same flash of direct knowledge, but now the great structure of the intellect has been built up through intervening ages and by its means the intuitive knowledge can descend to our daily life in full consciousness.
J. J. van der Leeuw, LL. D., *The Conquest of Illusion*, p. 46.
[5]) W. Hazlitt, *Lectures on the English Comic Writers*, p. 163.

reason : "De menigvuldige gegevens, die met 't moederschap samenhangen.... zijn beslissend voor de vrouw, die nooit moeder wordt als voor haar, die dit wel wordt. Voor de laatste neemt 't moederschap zoozeer al haar krachten naar geest en lichaam in beslag, dat een kunstuiting iets van ondergeschikte orde zal moeten zijn." [1]) That the writing of a novel required the whole woman was confirmed by Charlotte Brontë after *Shirley* had been sent to the publishers : "You can write nothing of value unless you give yourself wholly to the theme...." [2])

Investigations, however, have proved that the female intellect is certainly not behind the male. Yet though countless women have retired into convents, where they could devote themselves to study and writing, only a single abbess is mentioned as the writer of the story of her convent. As far as education is concerned : the girls as well as the boys were taught philosophy and literature. Letters are preserved of intelligent women giving evidence of woman's education and of her literary powers. Only, the latter part of the seventeenth century was a period of neglect in this respect for "even in the highest ranks and in those situations which afforded the greatest facilities for mental improvement, the English women of that generation were decidedly worse educated than they have been at any other time since the revival of learning." [3]) It may also be stated here that some of the great literary men were of humble birth with hardly any learning at all and yet they knew how to push their way to fame and glory. As for Ellen Key's argument : not all women married and had children ; so we might expect a great number of unmarried authoresses.

A more acceptable argument is provided by Leslie Stephen, who, seeing that most lady-novelists began writing at a mature age, says : "these precedents may suggest that women, who have the gift, have been often kept back by the feminine virtue of

---

[1]) Ellen Key, *De misbruikte krachten der vrouw*. Vertaling van de Deensche brochure *Missbrukad Kwinnokraft*, door Ph. Wijsman, p. 12.
[2]) Letter from Charlotte Brontë to Mr. Williams, Aug. 29th 1849.
[3]) Th. B. Macaulay, *History of England*, Vol. I, p. 304.

diffidence."[1]) Women shrank from the judgment of the world, that would have condemned a lady-writer as being an unwomanly character. This is a most plausible reason and the biographies of lady-novelists offer plenty of material to confirm this theory.

Though women wove or embroidered heroic deeds of warriors, lives of saints, whole battles on tapestries, cushions, banners, in their hours of leisure, it would have been considered disgraceful, if they had published the outcome of their thoughts by means of books. "If a damsel had the least smattering of literature, she was regarded as a prodigy,"[2]) was the opinion in the seventeenth century. Mrs. H. G. Aldis in her article on *The Bluestockings* says: "During the first half of the eighteenth century English women had little education and still less educational status. It was considered 'unbecoming' for them to know Greek or Latin, almost immodest for them to be authors and certainly indiscrete te own the fact."[3]) People continued to cherish suchlike views till the middle of the nineteenth century. Fanny Burney puts the general opinion about lady-writers in the mouth of one of her personages: Mr. Harrat rebukes Cecilia, the heroine of the novel of this name, about the high bill of her bookseller, winding up with the words: "And let me counsel you to remember that a lady, whether so called from birth or only from fortune, should never degrade herself by being put on a level with writers and such sort of people."[4]) When Charlotte Brontë asked Southey's opinion about her wish to become an author, he answered on February 20th 1837: "Literature cannot be the business of a woman's life and it ought not to be. The more she is engaged in her proper duties, the less leisure will she have for it, even as an accomplishment and recreation."[5]) Charlotte Brontë makes one of her female characters say: "It appears to me that ambition, literary ambition especially, is not a feeling

---
[1]) Leslie Stephan, *Life of George Eliot*, Gh. IV. p. 52
[2]) Th. B. Macaulay, *History of England*, Vol. I. p. 304.
[3]) *Cambridge History of English literature*, Vol. XI, Ch. XV.
[4]) F. Burney, *Cecilia*, Bk. II, p. 179.
[5]) Letter from Southey to Charlotte Brontë, Feb. 20th, 1837.

to be cherished in the mind of a woman." [1]) When Charlotte Mary Yonge began to write "authorship was considered unladylike and a family-council consented to the publication of *Abbey Church* only on the condition, that she should not accept the pecuniary returns for any personal end." [2])

For fear of public opinion some of the female pioneers sought shelter under a pseudonym. When Miss Burney published her first novel, "she took the name of Grafton, and desired that letters addressed to her might be left at the Orange Coffee-house." [3]) Jane Austen's works appeared anonymously, which must be attributed to Jane's being "scrupulous about social sentiment," [4]) because in her days a woman who wrote a book was still considered as "overstepping the limitations of her sex." [5])

It was not only the pioneers, who veiled their names. Fifty years later the sisters Brontë also did so. Charlotte explains why they did it: "The ambiguous choice being dictated by a sort of conscientious scruple at assuming Christian names positively masculine, while we did not like to declare ourselves women because — without at that time suspecting that our mode of writing and thinking was not what is called 'feminine' — we had a vague impression that authoresses are liable to be looked on with prejudice ; we had noticed how critics sometimes use for their chastisement the weapon of personality, and for their reward, a flattery, which is not true praise." [6]) Even with regard to the anonymous publication of *Villette*, Charlotte writes to Mr. Smith of Messrs. Smith and Elder, the publishers, that if it should not injure the publisher's interest "she should be most thankful for the sheltering shadow of an incognito." [7]) In 1848 Mrs. Gaskell published her

---

[1]) Charlotte Brontë, *The Professor*, Tauchnitz ed., p. 200.
[2]) *Chambers' Cyclopaedia*, Vol. II, p. 535.
[3]) Th. B. Macaulay, *Critical and Historical Essays*, p. 676.
[4]) Goldwin Smith, *Life of Jane Austen*, p. 34.
[5]) ibid., p. 34.
[6]) Ellis Bell, *Wuthering Heights*, Biographical Notes by Currer Bell.
[7]) Mrs. E. C. Gaskell, *The Life of Charlotte Brontë*, Dent's ed., p. 364.

first novel *Mary Barton* under the pseudonym of Cotton Mather Mill Esq. "Mary Ann Evans was thirty-seven, when George Eliot was born", we read in *The Bookman* of Nov. 1919.

When it was discovered who the author of a newly published book was and she appeared to be a woman, this woman found fewer obstacles and less disdain than she had expected. People gradually began to see that the differences of character, temperament and endowment between men and women, which were often alleged as arguments why women ought not to appear in the field of letters, but should preserve their powers for domestic duties, might be turned to good account when women set to writing.

When Miss Burney's first novel appeared both Burke and Johnson loudly praised this pioneer. Burke ends his letter of praise with the words: "In an age distinguished by producing extraordinary women I hardly dare to tell you where my opinion would place you amongst them." [1]) Later on it is Sir Walter Scott and Macaulay who praise Jane Austen loudly. Scott wrote in his diary: "That young lady has a talent for describing the involvements of feelings and characters of ordinary life which is to me the most wonderful I ever met with." Macauly made the following entry about Jane Austen's novels in his: "There are in the world no compositions which approach nearer to perfection". In the preface to Fanny Burney's *Cecilia* the editor of Fanny's early diary, Miss Annie Raine Ellis, says that "it is impossible to doubt that to Frances Burney we owe in great measure the many admirable novels written by women. The discovery that a young and modest lady could write without causing horror to her friends and, while marrying her heroines, hindering her own marriage, must have had great influence upon the families of two ladies younger than Mad. D'Arblay, of Maria Edgeworth, born in 1767, and of Jane Austen, born in 1775, as well as upon themselves."

The opening lines of the article *On the Female Literature of*

---

[1]) Letter of Edmund Burke to Miss F. Burney, July 29, 1782.

the Present Age in the *New Monthly Magazine and Universal Register for March* 1829 pay homage to female activity: "There is no more delightful peculiarity of the literature of the present age than the worth and the brilliancy of its female genius. The full development of the intellect and imagination of women is her triumph of modern times...."

Mrs. Gaskell openly defends the writing of women as follows: "When a man becomes an author, it is merely a change of employment to him. He takes a portion of that time which has hitherto been devoted to some other study or pursuit; ....A woman's principal work in life is hardly left to her own choice; nor can she drop the domestic charges devolving on her as an individual, for the exercise of the most splendid talents that were ever bestowed. And yet she must not shrink from the extra responsibility implied by the very fact of her possessing such talents. She must not hide her gift in a napkin; it was meant for the use and service of others. In a humble and faithful spirit must she labour to do what is not impossible, or God would not have set her to do it." [1]

Though some authoresses may have followed their own inclinations to appear in the literary world, there were many others who were forced by circumstances to do so. Aphra Behn found herself compelled to make a living with her pen. Mrs. Inchbald, though she already wrote in her husband's lifetime, had to provide for herself by writing. She acknowledged this openly, speaking in the third person, in the preface of *The Simple Story:* "with the utmost detestation to the fatigue of inventing, a constitution suffering under a sedentary life, and an education confined to the narrow boundaries prescribed by her sex, it has been her fate to devote a tedious seven years to the unremitting labour of literary productions." Though she is willing to attribute her success to Good Fortune, she continues in the first person: "There is a first cause to whom I cannot forbear to mention my obligations.

---

[1] Mrs. E. C. Gaskell, *The Life of Charlotte Brontë*, Dent's ed., p. 238.

.... Necessity, who being the mother of Invention gave me all my inspirations...." After her husband's death Mrs. Oliphant started novel-writing and because of her pecuniary difficulties wrote too many novels and so hurt her reputation as an author. On the death of their only son Mr. Gaskell advised his wife to write a novel as a means to get over the loss which she took so much to heart. George Eliot's talents would never have been displayed to the world but for the encouragement and stimulation given her by Mr. Lewes, while Mrs. Humphry Ward was always at work, writing articles, later on novels "to eke out the family income." [1]

Ever since women were free from the fetters which had so long prevented them from displaying their literary faculties, they have used their great gifts of observation, fantasy and intuition to create heroes, who, in their way, were not a whit inferior to the creations of male authors. The latter's conceptions of ideal knights, adventurers and knaves, were hardly ever the fruit of observation ; for those persons they simply drew open their imaginative powers, which to a great extent revealed and reflected their own mental dispositions and their mental reactions to what they had heard or read, or to relatively unimportant incidents they had experienced. Helped by fantasy they knew how to turn a sometimes unimportant event into an interesting story. Women were handicapped in this respect as their lives were less adventurous than those of men, and their experiences were chiefly limited to the domestic circle. Mrs. Ward avows this when she pronounces her view of the ultimate position of women-novelists : "....after all, women's range of material, even in the novel, is necessarily limited. There are a hundred subjects and experiences from which their mere sex debars them." [2] With the introduction of realistic novels, containing personages and incidents such as women too could observe, woman's literary activities were awaked together with the wish to compete with

---

[1] G. M. Trevelyan, *The Life of Mrs. Humphry Ward,* Ch. II, p. 26.
[2] ibid., Ch. IX, p. 168.

the male authors. Most of the authoresses before they entered upon their literary career were ardent readers and consequently well acquainted with the current types of heroes, and though they might take the prototype of their heroes from among the people of their immediate surroundings yet they could not help endowing them with traits that were fashionable for the moment. This is especially true of the first female venturers. It would appear that the latter, when writing, either had their eyes on some real person known to them, who might pass as an embodiment of certain desirable and admirable qualities, or that they simply ascribed to him these fashionable qualities, found in the heroes of whom they had read. So far from 'stripping their characters naked', they overlaid them with extraneous matter and the process did not make for naturalness. Later lady-novelists, while retaining the method, improved upon it and the result was a gallery of carefully drawn portraits of existing persons they had met. When in the beginning of the nineteenth century psychology became an acknowledged and popular branch of study, people began to pay more attention to the actions of a fellowman, the motives that gave rise to them and the circumstances under which they took place, and tried to explain every deed from the character of the person. Abundance of psychological insight was displayed by the lady-authors in the description of their heroes. For them the hero is not only the man in his relations to his fellow-men, in his attitude to the world, but also the man in his moments of mental solitude. Mrs. Humphry Ward expresses her ideas in her preface to the sixth London edition of *David Grieve* : "I am so made that I cannot picture a human being's development without wanting to know the whole, his religion as well as his actions. I cannot try to reflect my time without taking account of forces which are at least as real and living as any other forces, and have at least as much to do with the drama of human existence about me."

Now as it is difficult for anyone to understand the motives

of their own sex, it will hardly ever be given to them to comprehend a member of the opposite sex ; to follow them in their thoughts and dealings. So we may take for granted that men's heroines as well as women's heroes will betray a similar lack of reality and an equal share of romanticism. However, "les femmes lisent avec plus de vérité dans les hommes que les hommes dans les femmes" according to Eugène Forcade, whom Charlotte Brontë considered the best critic of her works. Women by their greater emotionality, their readier sympathy, and by the ease with which they imagine themselves in the place of another person, are able to read deeper into the characters under their observation, whilst their intuition often enables them to find out at once what is at the back of their actions. It has also been asserted that if a woman is able to draw manly characters naturally, contemporary novelists and critics are at a loss about the sex of the author. This was the case with Currer Bell and George Eliot. Such an author must be a woman with manly characteristics' to be able to understand the other sex so well.

The following chapters will show a succession of heroes of different kinds who succeeded in attracting and in holding the general interest during the period of their creation and even longer. It will be the present writer's task to treat each novelist separately by giving a short description of her life and the events that play an important part in it, and by quoting passages from her writings to show that the hero involuntarily reflects woman's position in society, her relation towards the other sex, and the intellectual development of woman. The writer feels justified in discussing only the prominent authoresses, each of them being a centre round which groups a collection of satellites, whose heroes imitate more or less the example of their guiding star.

CHAPTER III.

APHRA BEHN (1640—1689).

Aphra Behn was the first woman-novelist that contributed to the development of the novel, "the first to make use of incidents of real life in the service of fiction" [1]) and the first to earn her livelihood by her pen; the "George Sand of the Restoration" [2]) as Edmund Gosse calls her. She was born at Wye in Kent in 1640 and baptized on the 10th of June as the daughter of John and Amy Johnson. Later investigations have proved that her family name was Amis. After the death of her father, a London barber, an uncle took care of her and took her with him, intending to go to Surinam where he had been appointed governor. [3]) On his way there, however, he died. She continued the voyage, spent a short time in Surinam and returned to England in 1658. Shorty after she married Mr. Behn, a Dutchman by birth, and was presented at Court. Encouraged by the King, she described to him the colony of Surinam and the black prince Oroonoko, who was to be later on the hero of her first novel. After her husband's death she found herself in need of money. She turned for help to the Court, and was given work as a spy at Antwerp, but was not paid for her services. At last she saw herself compelled by pecuniary difficulties to earn her daily

---

[1]) W. Raleigh, *The English Novel*, p. 107.
[2]) E. Gosse in *Dictionary of National Biography* IV.
[3]) Montague Summers in his new collected edition of Mrs. Behn's works observes in his memoir of A. Behn, that it was her father himself, who, having been promised some important post, took his family to Surinam.
Aphra Behn herself says: "My father dy'd at Sea, and never arriv'd to possess the Honour design'd him, which was Lieutenant-general of six and thirty Islands, besides the Continent of Surinam, nor the advantages he hoped to reap by them.
Montague Summer's ed., p. 177.

bread. She started writing, first dramas, afterwards novels, with so much success that she became a well-known figure in literary circles. The foundation of her literary career was perhaps formed by her being a woman of reading; she especially liked the French romances of her time, among which Mlle. de Scudéry's *Le Grand Cyrus* seems to have taken up a foremost place. She died on April 16 1689 and was buried in Westminster Abbey, an honour which is not shared by any other female novelist. Her tombstone bears the following lines :

> "Here lies a Proof that Wit can never die
> Defence enough against Mortality."

This extraordinary woman lived in one of the most decadent periods of English history. The immorality of Charles the Second's Court is well-known. Aphra Behn had been an eye-witness of it, as she had been an eye-witness of the mental reaction leading to the Restoration, when Puritan tyranny and narrow-mindedness were replaced by a longing to enjoy life again. The Court set an example in giving festivals and entertainments. The refined French manners and fashions it had brought with it from its exile found ready imitation among all classes of the population. However, the newly restored liberty soon degenerated into licentiousness and also in this the Court and the fashionable world led the way.

The heroic romance with its ideal cavalier-hero and the picaresque novel were the leading 'vehicles' of literature at that time. A spirit of rivalry of these heroes of unreality arose which was the outcome of the dissatisfaction with the new moral or immoral regime, and represented the needs of the nation. Perhaps it was this spirit that induced Aphra Behn to write *Oroonoko*; it may be her moral ego revolted against the frivolous emptiness of the lives of her generation, and caused in her a dislike to all the vice, sin and corruption of which she had been such a close witness. In her plays and short stories she satisfied the general taste, and showed herself a real child of her time. Alexander

Pope refers to her loose language in his *Imitations of Horace* where he says:

"The stage how loosely does Astraea tread,
Who fairly puts all characters to bed." [1])

In her first novel she pictured her hero as the ideal of her mind. She did not want "to entertain her Readers with the adventures of a feigned Hero," [2]) but described a living being whom she makes the mouthpiece of her feelings on morality and religion. He was the representative of Man in "the first state of Innocence, before Man knew how to sin." [3]) When she was in Surinam she observed the Negro-slaves, and this made this conception still clearer. Back in England, she soon met in her reading descriptions of the ideal courtier, the heroic temper of the honest old Cavalier, who differed so much from those whom she met at the Court. The negro Oroonoko is the representative of this ideal cavalier. He was the perfection of male beauty, which she describes in the minutest detail. "He was pretty tall, but of a shape the most exact that can be fancy'd ....His face was not of that brown, rusty Black, which most of that Nation are, but a perfect Ebony.... His eyes were the most awful that cou'd be seen and very piercing; the White of 'em being like Snow, as were his Teeth. His nose was rising and 'Roman' instead of 'African' and flat: His mouth the finest shaped that could be seen; far from those great turn'd Lips which are so natural to the rest of the Negroes. The whole proportion and Air of his Face was so nobly and exactly formed, that bating his Colour, there could be nothing in Nature more beautiful, agreeable and handsome.... His Hair came down to his Shoulders.... Nor did the Perfections of his Mind come short of those of his Person; for his Discourse was admirable upon almost any subject...." [4]) He spoke the three modern

---

[1]) A. Pope, *The Imitations of Horace*, Bk. II, line 290-291.
[2]) *The Works of Aphra Behn*, ed. by Montague Summers, Vol. V., p. 129.
[3]) ibid., p. 131. [4]) ibid., p. 136.

languages fluently,[1]) was a clever mathematician and astrologer,[2]) was well up in history, even knew of the troubles that were raging in Europe at that time.[3]) Moreover, he was endowed with the noble virtues of the Knights of the Round Table: courage and bravery, for "at the age of 17 he was one of the most expert captains and bravest soldiers, that ever saw the field of Mars."[4]) He possessed generosity, tenderness, and respect for women, so that he made Imoinda a good and loving husband. In short "the most illustrious Courts could not have produced a braver man, both for greatness of courage and mind."[5]) He did not believe in a God, could not conceive the doctrine of Trinity, nor form an idea of what 'belief' is. Here the authoress displays her thoughts on religion, for which she is often declared to be 'a freethinker'. She wants to demonstrate that even without religion a man can be the perfection of morality. The captain of the Slaveship swore by God to land Oroonoko in the next port[6]); yet in spite of his oath he kept him on board and sold him. Oroonoko rightly called out on leaving the ship, when he was sold: " 't is worth my sufferings to gain a knowledge both of you and the God by whom you swear."[7]) For him 'Honour was the first Principle of Nature that was to be obeyed.[8]) Oroonoko's honour was such as he had never violated himself in his life, because it would have rendered him "contemptible and despised by all brave and honest men."[9]) To Oroonoko honour was the greatest judge of morality. This judge which some call conscience, and which William Law in *His serious Call* calls Faith, is the inner light, the direct voice of God to man, the feeling of approval or dissatisfaction in the inner self of one's own deeds and those of others. Rousseau expresses it by saying: "L'homme naturel est tout pour lui ; il est l'unité numérique, l'entier absolu, qui n'a rapport qu'à lui-même ou à son semblable."[10]) Oroonoko's opinion was: "The man of no Honour

---

[1]) ibid., 136. [2]) ibid., 167. [3]) ibid., 135. [4]) ibid., 134. [5]) ibid., 135
[6]) ibid., 163. [7]) ibid., 166. [8]) ibid., 164. [9]) ibid., 164.
[10]) J. J. Rousseau, *Emile*, Tome I, Livre I, p. 15.

suffers every moment the scorn and contempt of the honester World and dies every day ignominously in his Fame, which is more valuable than Life." [1])

Aphra Behn hated a religion which is mere outward show, partyhatred and formulas. It does not matter, whether it is Honour, Duty, Conscience or Fear of a higher Being, that leads Man to Morality, so long as he is led there. Among Oroonoko's people "religion wou'd destroy that Tranquillity they possess by Ignorance." [2])

She also attacked the distribution of well-paid and honourable posts, which were too much reserved for the higher classes, whilst no regard was paid to able and capable people among the lower. Macaulay drew attention to this evil : "Whoever could make himself agreeable to the prince, or could secure the good offices of the mistress, might hope to rise in the world without rendering any service to the government, without being even known by sight to any minister of state. This courtier got a frigate, and that a company.... If the king notified his pleasure that a briefless lawyer should be made a judge, or that a libertine baronet should be made a peer, the gravest councillors, after a little murmuring, submitted." [3]) When Oroonoko's country was in danger and the ambassadors came to ask him to be their leader, he refused because of his grief for his bride, who had been sold by his grand-father. His answer was remarkable, for he advised them to choose "the bravest Man amongst 'em, let his Quality and Birth be what it wou'd. For, oh my Friends, it is not Titles that make Men brave or good or Birth that bestows Courage and Generosity...." [4])

In the natural Man, as he came from his Creator's hands, in the return to Nature, Aphra Behn saw the only escape from the corrupt laws, the hollow religion and the voluptuousness of her time. Rousseau expresses this idea : "Tout est bien, sortant

---

[1]) *The Works of A. Behn,* ed. by Montague Summers, Vol. V, p. 164
[2]) ibid., Vol. V, p. 132.
[3]) Th. B. Macaulay, *History of England,* Vol. I, p. 282.
[4]) Montague Summers, *The Works of Aphra Behn,* Vol. V, p. 158.

des mains de l'Auteur des choses ; tout dégénere entre les mains de l'homme." [1]) Oroonoko's cruel death may be a reflection of the cruelty displayed in the measures of repression after Monmouth's attempt to make himself king.

In creating Oroonoko Aphra Behn introduced a quite new hero into fiction: 'the noble savage' who may be partly traced back to the hero of chivalry, but with characteristics borrowed from real life. It is strongly to be doubted, if Mrs. Behn in taking a negro for her hero, intended to be the champion of the emancipation of slaves and "to awaken Christendom to the horrors of slavery."[2]) The condition of the slaves does not seem to have drawn much attention at that time. She probably intended rather to lay stress on the ideal state of man which had made such an impression upon her. Whether she may be considered a forerunner of Rousseau or is rightly to be called 'the grandmother of the French revolution' is another doubtful question. It is, of course, possible to infer this from the conception of the hero's life and to see with Professor Prinsen "in den neger Oroonoko, die weinig geloof er op na houdt en toch van een hooge zedelijkheid is, een voorlooper van de romanhelden uit de school van Rousseau." [3]) It is certain, however, that the novelist used her hero to point out existing evils, which Rousseau did with more force a hundred years afterwards, perhaps not foreseeing that the remedy of these evils was to be found in revolution. Her taking for her hero this original character, a negro, whose life and experiences she depicted in a manner very attractive to the general reader, "entitles her to claim a share in the attempt, faint and ineffective, that the later seventeenth century witnessed to bring romance into closer relation with contemporary life." [4])

---

[1]) J. J. Rousseau, *Emile*, Tome I, Livre I, p. 1.
[2]) W. L. Cross, *Development of the English Novel*, Ch. I, p. 20.
[3]) Dr. J. Prinsen, J.Lzn. *De Roman in de 18e eeuw in West-Europa*, p. 218.
[4]) W. Raleigh, *The English Novel*, Ch. IV, p. 109.

CHAPTER IV.

FRANCES BURNEY (1752—1840).

Aphra Behn's example had been followed by only a few contemporary lady-writers, and it was not until a hundred years afterwards that a woman again made an attempt at prose-writing.

At the time when Fanny Burney sent her first product into the world, the novel was not in a very flourishing condition. The great authors who had given a definite shape to the novel had died, but their heroes were still vivid in the minds of the then generation. No wonder that Fanny Burney's work created a stir. She followed the same method Richardson and Fielding had used in representing human beings and human conduct, — 'speaking from a full and ripe experience'. This woman introduced at the same time the real principle of the novel by applying it to ordinary life, the actual life that was going on around all her readers.

Frances Burney, born on the 13th of June 1752 at Lynn Regis in Norfolk, was the second daughter of Dr. Charles Burney, a well-known organist and music master. Her father settled in London, where he became acquainted with a group of distinguished people, who soon frequented his house. He did not pay the least attention to his daughter's education, not even sending her to school. Macaulay remarks : "Her brothers and sisters called her a dunce and even at the age of eight she did not know her letters." [1]) She was always present when her father was visited by his intellectual friends, sitting in a corner

---

[1]) Th. B. Macaulay, *Critical and Historical Essays*, p. 669.

of the drawing-room, unnoticed by the others. By this she had the great advantage of being able to watch and observe the people present. Raleigh observes that "she had a quite marvellous faculty of taking impressions of actual speech, manners and to a certain extent, character : that she had at any rate for a time, a corresponding faculty of expressing or at least reporting her impressions." [1]) This last faculty was in a very great measure cultivated by writing every week a letter to an old friend, Mr. Crisp, to whom she gave a description of persons and incidents. To this gentleman she owes much, as he corrected her way of writing, and explained to her the method of the great masters of literature. Macaulay observes that her intellect was not formed by reading, for "at the height of her fame she was unacquainted with the most celebrated works of Voltaire and Molière." [2]) Yet she must have been thoroughly acquainted with Richardson's masterworks, as her heroes were such faithful pictures of 'the perfect gentleman.' Acquainted with the original hero, and living in a period that was not far removed from the first outburst of sentimentality, whilst "from the atmosphere of her own day she acquired the habit of the ever-ready tear and the lavish display of feeling," [3]) she must have applied with clear judgment the characteristics of Sir Charles Grandison to the persons she watched.

In 1778 at the age of twenty-six she published her first novel, a considerable time after finishing a sketch *Caroline Evelyn*, which may have been the foundation of Evelina. This product was burnt by her stepmother. As after her first success she came in contact with prominent literary figures and met almost every person of importance between the years 1778 and 1791, it might have been expected that the hero of her second novel was a more natural type ; but, though somewhat less staunch in his love for the heroine, he is again an image of Sir Charles.

---

[1]) W. Raleigh, *The English Novel*, p. 152.
[2]) Th. B. Macaulay, *Critical and Historical Essays*, p. 670.
[3]) Legouis and Cazamian, *A History of English Literature*, Vol. 11, Bk. IV, Ch. V, p. 241.

Frances Burney's five years at the Court as one of the keepers of the Queen's robes prevented her from writing when at the top of her fame. After her marriage to a French refugee, General D'Arblay, she published two more novels, being forced to do so by the loss of her husband's fortune. She died in 1840.

For the discussion of her heroes only the first two novels will be considered, as Fanny Burney's reputation as a novelist is founded on *Evelina* published in 1778 and *Cecilia* in 1882.

The hero, with whom the heroine of her first novel fell in love on the very day she met him for the first time, was Lord Orville, a man of "about twenty-six years old, extremely handsome," [1] of so gentle and so elegant manners, that they at once engaged esteem," [2] whose character was "quiet and reserved" [3] and "whose rank was his least recommendation, his understanding and his manners being far more distinguished."[4] He was pleased when he could render a service and always addressed people of every standing with the same politeness, without making distinction, being as modest "as if he had never mixed wit the great and was totally ignorant of every qualification he possessed." [5] When later on he met Evelina in far inferior company to that in which he was first introduced to her, he addressed and treated her "with the same politeness and attention with which he had always honoured her." [6] The people who accompanied her forced her to ask him for the use of his carriage, to which he consented as a matter of course. Being very much ashamed of their behaviour, she wrote him a letter of apology, which he answered with a note which pleased her at first. On a second reading, however, she grew very indignant at his impertinence. Her fosterfather, whom she told of this letter, concluded that "he must certainly have been intoxicated" [7] when he wrote it. This is the blot on the hero's character, which, however, will appear to be no blot at all. The heroine

---

[1]) Frances Burney, *Evelina,* Dent's ed., p. 25.
[2]) ibid., p. 67.   [3]) ibid., p. 220.   [4]) ibid., p. 28.   [5]) ibid., p. 106.
[6]) ibid., p. 222.   [7]) ibid., p. 249.

met him again at Bath and was deeply in love with "all that is amiable in man," [1]) when he adressed her "with a smile that indicated pleasure and eyes that sparkled with delight." [2]) He continued to be the noble, benevolent man he had been from the beginning: "who," — Evelina wrote to her stepfather —, "keeps to my side all the way we go; who, when we read, marks the passages most worthy to be noticed, draws out my sentiments and favours me with his own." [3]) When he thought that she had a secret meeting in the garden with one Mr. Macartney he showed his displeasure and disapproval clearly. "He did not again offer me his hand, but walked silent and slow by my side, his countenance much altered," [4] the heroine complained. When it happened again, he apologized to her "for being, just then, at the same place." [5]) He expressed a wish to be her friend, her brother, that he might have a right to protect her, and ended by falling in love with her. Upon his knees he proposed to her in the most exaggerated words, in keeping with the period in which the novelist lived: "I revere you! I esteem and I admire you above all human beings! You are the friend to whom my soul is attached as to its better half! You are the most amiable, the most perfect of women! and you are dearer to me than language has the power of telling." [6]) She inquired after the two letters, but he assured her, "he had never received, nor heard of any letter," [7]) with which explanation she was contented. Though she tried to make him understand that she was not worthy of his love, because she was an outcast, he assured her: "my heart is your's and I swear to you an attachment eternal.... So firm is my conviction." [8]) To Mrs. Selwynn, who told him the story of Evelina's life, he answered that he was "willing, nay, eager, that the [our] union should take place." [9])

From these citations it will appear that Orville in his conduct remains the same constant, noble, virtuous man, a worthy descendant

---

[1]) ibid., p. 259. [2]) ibid., p. 259. [3]) ibid., p. 273. [4]) ibid., p. 276.
[5]) ibid.   [6]) ibid., p. 326. [7]) ibid.   [8]) ibid., p. 342. [9]) ibid., p. 343.

of his illustrious ancestor Grandison. Dibelius rightly states that he is : von höchsten Richardsonschen Tugend." [1]) Hazlitt's judgment is not favourable, for he calls him "a condescending suit of clothes." [2]) When Orville pronounces his opinion about the heroine in her presence to Sir Clement Willoughby we may safely call him a prig. The reader is kept in the dark about his daily occupations and his ambitions; he only gets acquainted with the hero's attitude towards the heroine. On the last page of the book he is still the same character as on the first.

Mortimer Delville, the hero of the second novel, was "tall and finely formed; his features, though not handsome, were full of expression; and a noble openness of manners and address spoke the elegance of his education, and the liberality of his mind" [3]); in him "sincerity and vivacity joined with softness and elegance." [4]) The heroine soon fell in love with him, for "his character, upon every opportunity of showing it, rose in her opinion, and his disposition and manners had a mingled sweetness and vivacity that rendered his society attractive, and his conversation spirited." [5]) His mother's fondness of him "flowed not from relationship, but from his worth and character." [6]) For his father he was "not only the first object of his affection, but the chief idol of his pride...., the only support of his ancient name and family." [7]) At one time he was accused of having a mistress, but it turned out to be the result of a coincidence. He fell in love with Cecilia, but considered her beneath him in rank. This hindrance to his love affected him so intensely that he fell ill, and the doctors spoke of a mental disease. He betrayed his love to the heroine, though he was determined that "no human being.... should know, should even suspect the situation of his mind." [8]) In very tender language he spoke of his love, but also explained why he could not marry her. "My honour in the honour

---

[1]) W. Dibelins, *Englische Romankunst*, Band II, Kap. 9.
[2]) W. Hazlitt, *Sketches and Essays*, p. 181.
[3]) Frances Burney, *Cecilia*, Vol. I, Bk. II, p. 147.
[4]) ibid., p. 165. [5]) ibid., Bk. III, p. 232. [6]) Vol. II, Bk. VI, p. 6.
[7]) ibid., p. 6. [8]) ibid., p. 56.

of my family is bound !.... that forbids my aspiring to the first of women, but by an action that with my own family would degrade me for ever." [1]) He determined "to undergo an instant of even exquisite torture, in preference to a continuance of such lingering misery" [2]) and to leave England. Though he was firmly resolved to do so "to escape her neighbourhood," [3]) he stood quite unexpectedly before her when she was staying with a friend. "Delville instantly flew to her...., and he poured forth at her feet the most passionate acknowledgments." [4]) He persuaded her to consent "to an immediate and secret marriage," [5]) for now he had to confess that his parents would never consent to their union." [6]) She refused to accept this proposal, which for him was "the sole barrier between himself and perpetual misery." [7]) When he wrote her a letter to tell that as soon as he was married he was sure his parents would receive his bride, she consented. After a vehement quarrel with her son and a bad illness proceeding from it, his mother gave her consent and the marriage was contracted in privacy. His father refused to hear of it, but all was settled after the heroine had been taken seriously ill.

What has been said of the hero of the first novel with regard to his life in the world, apart from his attitude towards the heroine, also holds good for the hero of the second. He only makes a less pleasant impression by his love-affair. He, "a scion of a proud, ancient, penniless family," [8]) is "a perfect diplomatist in the art of lovemaking." [9]) Notwithstanding his proposals are clothed in the most sentimental language, this language "even of a young man making love, must have been simpler than that of Mr. Delville." [10]) The pity is only for himself, he does not care in the least what blow he deals the object of his admiration. His love is constant, but betrays a great portion of egoism, though

---

[1]) ibid., p. 56. [2]) ibid., p. 57. [3]) ibid., p. 61. [4]) ibid., p. 89.
[5]) ibid., p. 98. [6]) ibid., p. 98. [7]) ibid., p. 98.
[8]) W. Raleigh, *The English Novel*, p. 259.
[9]) W. Hazlitt, *Sketches and Essays*, p. 181.
[10]) O. Elton, *A Survey of English Literature*, 1780—1830, Vol. I, p. 177.

this must be considered in connection with the sentimental effect it produces. In view of all his dealings, his language and his love, the present writer can but class him among the offspring of Richardson's hero, "the prince of coxcombs, whose eye was never once taken from his own person and his own virtues." [1]

---

[1] W. Hazlitt, *Lectures on the English Comic Writers*, p. 158.

CHAPTER V.

CLARA REEVE (1799—1807).

When Walpole in 1764 published his *Castle of Otranto* he opened the line of novelists, who, incited by a growing interest in the Middle Ages and fostered by a longing for the supernatural, took up their places among the adherents of romanticism. They form the romantic school of prose fiction, of which Clara Reeve is the first female representative.

She was the daughter of the Reverend William Reeve, rector of Freston and Kerston in Suffolk. Her father taught her all the learning she knew. She was greatly interested in English history, and in the biographical preface to *The Old English Baron* it says that she was a lady of high accomplishments and various talents. Of her life there is little to tell. After her father's death she went with her mother to Colchester, where she lived a very retired life, having little contact with the world, so that the heroes she created are characters which she can only have formed by reading. She confesses in the preface of her first novel, that her story is "the literary offspring of the *Castle of Otranto*. However, if we may cite Sir Walter Scott's saying, the hero of this novel is the creation of "a man of the world, who knew the world like a man," [1] and who knew how to make an interesting lifelike picture of the principal character. "Théodore est le jeune cavalier sans peur et sans reproche, protecteur des dames en détresse, tel qu'on le voyait dans les anciens romans de chevalerie et prototype du jeune héros chez la plupart des romanciers de ce

---

[1] Sir Walter Scott, *Lives of the Novelists*. p. 204.

genre." [1]) Clara Reeve made the hero of her firstling, which she wrote at the mature age of fifty-one and to which she owed her reputation, an imitation of the heroic cavalier, but at the same time the lineal descendant of Richardson's hero. Alice Killen rightly observes : "Si elle se donna comme tâche de continuer à marcher dans la voie que Walpole avait tracée, elle n'en fut pas moins en même temps une descendante littéraire de Richardson, dont elle a toute la sentimentalité fade." [2])

Edmund Twyford, who was generally considered the son of a cottager, was a young man of "uncommon merit" [3]) who "from his childhood attracted the affection of all that knew him." [4]) He was educated by Lord FitzOwen, whose sons were his playfellows. When Sir Philip Harclay came to see Lord FitzOwen he at once liked Edmund so much, that he offered to adopt him. Edmund's heart, however, was "unalterably attached to the house and family" [5]) and he wanted to spend his life in his benefactor's service. His character was most amiable : "he was modest, yet intrepid ; gentle and courteous to all, frank and unreserved to those that loved him ; discreet and complaisant to those who hated him ; generous and compassionate to the distress of his fellowcreatures in general ; humble, but not servile, to his patron and superiors." [6]) Yet the eldest son did not like him and, helped by his friends, tried to make him suspect in his father's eyes. He had to appear before Lord FitzOwen to account for some accusation. The younger son who came to fetch him loved him very much and before returning home, they promised each other "to preserve the same constant friendship." [7]) The sentimentality of the period justifies the scene that followed, which to the eyes of a modern reader must seem rather exaggerated seeing that it concerns boys of about seventeen. They knelt down and "invoked the supreme to witness to their friendship and implored his blessing upon it ; they then rose up

---

[1]) Alice M. Killen, *Le Roman Terrifiant*, Partie I, Ch. I, p. 4.
[2]) ibid., p. 2.
[3]) Clara Reeve, *The Old English Baron*, p. 12.
[4]) ibid., p. 12.   [5]) ibid., p. 14.   [6]) ibid., p. 20.   [7]) ibid., p. 32.

and embraced each other while tears of cordial affection bedewed their cheeks." [1]) The accusations appeared to be false and the baron wished to put an end to these attacks on Edmund's innocense and courage. He asked him to spend three successive nights in the haunted part of the castle. Edmund was quite willing to undertake this to show his courage. "I have not wilfully offended God or man; I have, therefore, nothing to fear," [2]) he said. In the haunted chamber he had a strange dream, in which the secret of his birth was revealed to him. He set out to Sir Philip Barclay, an old friend of his father's, and asked him to help him to claim his birthright. Before his departure his benefactor's daughter had told him that somebody had asked her hand in marriage, but Edmund had advised her not to accept this proposal and to wait for a friend of his, whose "birth was [is] noble, his degree and fortune uncertain" [3]) and whose ambition was [is] first to deserve and then to obtain it." [4]) When he had returned as her equal in birth he asked her hand of her father, who consented if Edmund really loved his daughter. His answer is worthy of Sir Charles Grandison himself: "I never loved any woman but her, and, if I am so unfortunate as to be refused her, I will not marry at all.... Your family are the whole world to me. Give me you lovely daughter.... What is title or fortune, if I am deprived of the society of those I love." [5]) When Emma was asked, if she loved Edmund, "he trembled and leaned upon William's shoulder to support himself." [6]) He asked Lord FitzOwen and Sir Philip to live with them, but both preferred to live in the neighbourhood and to leave the young couple together. The cottage in which his fosterparents had lived till then, he offered them as a present and asked them to visit his wife and himself as much as they liked.

Clara Reeve admits her indebtedness to Walpole for the *Old English Baron,* but hers is not a mere imitation of this author's hero.

His faultless character, his conduct and his sentimentality reflect Richardson's ideal and the period in which the novel was

---
[1]) ibid., p. 32.   [2]) ibid., p. 35.   [3]) ibid., p. 64.   [4]) ibid., p. 64.
[5]) ibid., p. 142.   [6]) ibid., p. 142.

written. Though he is rather too weak-hearted for a youth of his age, he is at the same time an enterprising man who carries out his projects to attain his end. In his energy and courage as well as in his mysterious birth he resembles Tom Jones, Fielding's hero. In his love he is again the sentimental hero who cannot live without the object of his affections. As there is total absence of personal description, the reader gets to know the hero by the moralising way in which he repeatedly expresses himself, which is more in keeping with the prevailing customs of the novelist's own period than with those of the fifteenth century, in which the story is supposed to have taken place.

CHAPTER VI.

ANN RADCLIFFE (1764—1823).

The literary mood of the period still favoured the supernatural, the truly mysterious. Mrs. Radcliffe perfected what Walpole began and Clara Reeve continued: the novel of terror. Her heroes, however, do not show improvement on those created by her predecessors.

Ann Ward was born in London on the 9th of July 1764. She was the daughter of a tradesman and spent her life in peace and quiet at her father's house till the age of twenty-two, when she married William Radcliffe, a barrister, afterwards editor of *The English Chronicle*. His journalistic work kept him very busy and did not leave him much time to occupy himself with his young wife. She filled her solitary evenings by trying to write a novel and succeeded very well in the attempt. Only two years after her marriage her first literary product appeared. She was a great reader. Alice Killen states that she was "une liseuse infatigable de Gray, Collins, de Thomson. Elle connaissait l'Arioste, elle fera des emprunts à Rousseau et à Madame de Genlis. Mais Shakespeare fut son maître."[1] She must have been very well acquainted with Richardson's and Fielding's novels as well, for their influence is distinctly noticeable in her heroes. Considering her retired life and limited knowledge and experience, she can only have acquired the motives and characters of her novels by reading, which is confirmed by Sir Walter Raleigh when he observes: "the ignorance of the world at the

---

[1] A. M. Killen, *Le Roman Terrifiant*, Bk. II, p. 18.

time when she wrote was complete and many-sided. Human character she knew not from observation, but from dreams." [1]) The novel which claims our attention (as the hero, Valancourt, swerves somewhat from the current type found in her other novels) is *The Mysteries of Udolpho*, which appeared in 1794. "Nobody can find any fault with them, for nobody knows anything about them. They are described very handsome and quite unmeaning and inoffensive. 'Her heroes have no character at all'," [2]) is William Hazlitt's bold opinion of these characters. "Nur ein einziger Tom Jones findet sich im Kreise dieser unfehlbaren Männlichkeit: 'Valancourt'," [3]) Dibelius says.

This Valancourt was "the younger son of an ancient family of Gascony" and "was educated in all the accomplishments of his age," [4]) so that "his genius and accomplishments would amply supply deficiency of his inheritance." [5]) He had become an officer, for which profession he was eminently suited in the opinion of his brother, on whom he was dependent. The reader makes his acquaintance, when he is wandering among the Pyrenees and is hurt by a shot in his arm. St. Aubert, the heroine's father, who was struck by his "chevalierlike air and open countenance" [6]) when he met him for the first time, had an opportunity of observing him and saw "a frank and generous nature, full of ardour, highly susceptible of whatever is grand and beautiful, but impetuous, wild and somewhat romantic." [7]) He fell in love with Emily and his proposal reminds the reader of the sentimental hero; he spoke to her of "the many anxious hours," [8]) he had passed. When all was arranged for his wedding, the preparations were used for the wedding of Emily's aunt, to which feast Valancourt had also been invited. Our hero, instead of venting his indignation, which every young man in his circumstances would have done, "endeavoured to check his

---

[1]) W. Raleigh, *The English Novel*, p. 228.
[2]) W. Hazlitt, *Sketches and Essays*, p. 180.
[3]) W. Dibelius, *Englische Romankunst*, p. 298.
[4]) A. Radcliffe, *The Mysteries of Udolpho*, p. 134.
[5]) ibid., p. 134.   [6]) ibid., p. 36.   [7]) ibid., p. 47.   [8]) ibid., p. 116.

concern."[1]) His bride had to go with her new uncle and aunt to Italy. Valancourt had quarrelled with this aunt and was not allowed to see his Emily again. At night he came to see her under her window, but instead of comforting the girl, he, "relapsing into despondency, again felt for himself and lamented again this cruel separation."[2]) This egotistic grief bears a striking resemblance to the sorrow of Delville, Frances Burney's hero. Valancourt differs from Delville in so far, that later on he acknowledged, that he was "a wretch...." and "ought to have shown the fortitude of man."[3]) He could not follow her to Italy, for he had to join his regiment in Paris. In the beginning he nursed his grief in solitude and his "reserved and thoughtful manners were a kind of tacit censure"[4]) on the manners of his brother-officers, who teased and ridiculed him. This he could not endure and "soon frequented the most gay and fashionable circles of Paris,"[5]) where he seemed to forget his Emily. His small income was not sufficient to pay for this expensive way of living and our hero, "in consequence of accumulated debts, was thrown into confinement."[6]) When Valancourt's life took this turn, it was the influence of Tom Jones that inspired Ann Radcliffe. His Paris life justified Montoni's refusing Emily to have intercourse with Valancourt any more. He was very remorseful of his conduct when he saw Emily, the sight of whom "had renewed all the ardour with which he first loved her."[7]) The words with which he took leave of Emily prove the nobility of his character : "I resign you, Emily, and will endeavour to find consolation in considering that though I am miserable, you, at least, may be happy."[8]) "Though his passions had been seduced, his heart was not depraved,"[9]) and with great energy "he emancipated himself from the bondage of vice."[10]) In the end he was accepted again as Emily's lover.

The conception of this hero clearly shows traces of the prototype

---

[1]) ibid., p. 164. [2]) ibid., p. 178. [3]) ibid., p. 184. [4]) ibid., p. 336.
[5]) ibid., p. 336. [6]) ibid., p. 369. [7]) Bk. II, p. 216. [8]) ibid., p. 217.
[9]) ibid., p. 369. [10]) ibid., p. 369.

in Richardson, to which Tom Jones' characteristics have been added, while some of the hero's experiences betray imitation of Walpole's hero. His character is spoilt by the introduction of Fielding's motives. That Valancourt is soon attracted by the pleasures of the Parisian circles and that owing to his intercourse with wealthy friends he gets involved in pecuniary difficulties, which even lead to his imprisonment, does not turn him into a bad character. But his forgetting Emily is blameworthy "in a young man of noble principles and exalted sentiments after such a long intimacy and such a series of incidents tending to give permanency to his passion and stability to his character." [1])

Mrs. Radcliffe does not make any attempt at character-development. The hero is always a young lover, a noble, generous gentleman of high birth, with whom the heroine falls in love because of his amiable manners and captivating appearance. Valancourt, though led astray from the path of virtue, is aware of his fault in due time. This is the worst flaw in the character of any of the heroes, in whom a resemblance to Richardson's paragon of manly virtue can be traced.

---

[1]) *Monthly Review,* Sept.—Dec. 1794, p. 281.

CHAPTER VII.

ELIZABETH INCHBALD (1753—1821).

This lady-novelist was born on Oct. 15th 1753 at Standingfield near Bury St. Edmunds, and was the daughter of a poor Roman-Catholic farmer. She did not attend any school, she had no governess, and suffered from a pronounced stammer. The art of reading she acquired somehow, and she read everything she could lay hold on, forming in this way the foundation of her literary career. In spite of her imperfection of speech she had an eager wish to become an actress. She often attended performances in the Bury-theatre, the chief actor of which was her earliest hero.

When nineteen years old she visited London, where, at her sister's house, she made the acquaintance of her future husband, Mr. Joseph Inchbald, an actor about seventeen years her senior. Notwithstanding her marriage with this Protestant, she remained a staunch Roman-Catholic all her life. She succeeded in becoming an actress and in her stage-career met Mrs. Siddons, who encouraged her in her literary studies. At Edinburgh she started studying French, which language was perfected by a stay at Paris. Though a married woman, she fell in love with Mrs. Siddon's brother, John Philip Kemble, at whose instigation she began to write her novel, taking Kemble for her hero. It is supposed, that after her husband's sudden death, she expected that Kemble would ask her to become his wife and that in her disappointment, she turned her hero into the harsh, rigid egotist of the second part of her first novel. It may also be that she saw his real character and rejected his suit.

During the last forty years of her life she lived in London, working hard and living economically on the proceeds of her writings till she died in 1821.

Though she wrote many dramas, some of which were performed on the stage, she is best-known in literature for her first novel, *A Simple Story*, published in 1791. This very original woman took for her hero, as is said, the man that made such a deep impression on her· and by creating this character she created a type of hero unknown until then : the Roman-Catholic priest. "Lord Elmwood (Dorriforth), der starke, feste, ruhige und energisch wollende Mann mit seiner kolossalen Selbstbeherrschung ist ohne Tradition im Englischen Roman," [1] Dibelius rightly observes.

He was "bred at St. Omer's in all the scholastic rigour of that college and was by education and the solemn vows of his order a Roman-Catholic priest." [2] The authoress describes his personal appearance in detail : "his figure was tall and elegant ; but his face, except a pair of dark, bright eyes, a set of white teeth, and a graceful arrangement in his clerical curls of brown hair, had not one feature to excite admiration." [3] "On his countenance his thoughts were portrayed ; and as his mind was enriched with every virtue that could make it valuable, so was his face adorned with every expression of those virtues." [4] She perfects her hero's picture by giving an insight into his character. Though he was "by nature and more from education of a serious, thinking and philosophic turn of mind," [5] he was very obstinate. His obstinacy, had it not been that "religion and some contrary virtues were weighed heavily in the balance, would have frequently degenerated into implacable stubbornness." [6] When thirty years old he was entrusted with the guardianship of a friend's only daughter. His narrow mind was incapable of understanding his ward's character and temperament and he regarded

---

[1] W. Dibelius, *Englische Romankunst*, Band II, p. 20.
[2] E. Inchbald, *A Simple Story*, Baudrey's European Library, p. 1.
[3] ibid., p. 2.   [4] ibid., p. 2.   [5] ibid., p. 162.   [6] ibid., p. 36.

her "in the light of friendship only."[1]) He quarrelled with one of his ward's many admirers and slapped his face, which deed made him very miserable afterwards, because he had "stained the sacred character, the dignity of his profession."[2]) The duel that might have resulted from this insult, but from which he was exempt as a priest, betrays the influence of his prototype Grandison. Through the death of a relative he became Lord Elmwood and now he asked dispensation from his priestly vows in order to be able to marry. He married his ward, who had been in love with him from the beginning in spite of many apparent love-affairs with others. The ring he put on her finger on the wedding-day was 'a mourning ring'. Whether this was a bad omen or not, the second part of the book, undoubtedly bearing on her opinion of Kemble after her husband's death, shows that the marriage had not turned out to be 'the union for life'. Dorriforth, "the pious, the good, the tender Dorriforth had become a hard-hearted tyrant,"[3]) "an example of implacable rigour and injustice"[4]) through his wife's misconduct during his stay in the West-Indies. Being a Roman-Catholic, he could not divorce her, but he did not want to have anything to do with her and revenged her infidelity on her innocent child by refusing to see it. After his wife's death he allowed his daughter to live with him in the same house, but was not inclined to have any intercourse with her. One day he met her by chance, but he remained implacable. He threw off his disguise of harshness when he heard how his daughter had fallen into a trap, set by one of her admirers Now he was "willing to prove himself a father."[5]) Together with the man who wanted to marry her, he set out to the rescue, after which father and daughter were reconciled.

Mrs. Inchbald's writing presents a great contrast to that of contemporary lady-novelists, because she succeeded in creating in Dorriforth a man "who has a very stately opinion of himself,

---

[1]) ibid., p. 39. [2]) ibid., p. 57. [3]) ibid., p. 158. [4]) ibid., p. 157.
[5]) ibid., p. 254.

but has spirit and passion." [1]) Through his noble qualities and virtues he is a lineal descendant of Grandison, but endued with such life-like qualities as up till then no hero of female invention had been. By his unreasonable obstinacy he forfeits the reader's sympathy, but it is this very obstinacy that makes him a more natural being. It must be ascribed to the novelist's varied life, her coming in contact with people of different kinds as well as to her intuition, that she saw through a sympathetic outward appearance into the real character. Though her hero's life is only treated with regard to the love-interest, *A Simple Story* contains the strongest situation that had yet appeared in the English novel — the conflict between religious prejudice and love." [2])

---

[1]) W. Hazlitt, *Sketches and Essays*, p. 181.
[2]) W. L. Cross, *Development of the English Novel*, Ch. III, p. 88.

CHAPTER VIII.

MARIA EDGEWORTH (1767—1849).

The heroes of the novels which Maria Edgeworth wrote at the beginning of her literary career are again an improvement on the still reigning type. The authoress is the first to draw attention to national characteristics. This remarkable woman was born at Black Bourton near Oxford on the first of January 1767. She was a daughter of Richard Edgeworth, a great admirer of Rousseau and his theories on education and owner of a large estate at Edgeworthstown in Ireland. As a child of six she went to Ireland. When she returned to England she spent some years at a school at Derby, afterwards attending a more advanced school in London and went back to Ireland in 1782 when she was fifteen years old. She helped her father, who had married for the fourth time and had a large family, in writing business-letters, and was always present, when he received his tenants. So she had ample opportunity to get acquainted with the Irish. It is on her representation of Irish character that her fame is based. Sir Walter Scott admired her openly in his general preface to the 1829 edition of the *Waverley novels,* expressing a hope that what she did for Ireland he might be able to do for Scotland.

She was very fond of her father, who always meddled with her writing and forced her to pour her novels into a mould in accordance with his theories on education. His moralising influence is especially felt in her treatment of the hero with regard to the girl the hero has fallen in love with. The hero always inquires what education the girl has received and when a mother misconducted herself at some time, he thinks it impossible to marry her daughter. Her last novel *Helen*, written after her father's death, does not deal with Ireland and the hero is no longer a paragon of morality, for he cannot be persuaded to give up the object of his love, whatever may be alleged against or said of her. Miss Edgeworth died at Edgeworthstown on May 22nd 1849 at the age of eighty-two. Though during her long life she witnessed many important events in history (the whole French revolution and the Napoleonic period with its consequences for England, the troubles during the first half of the century in her native country, such as the Rebellion of 1798, the Union and the Famine), her heroes never refer by a single word to any of these events.

It will be sufficient for our purpose to consider a novel, written under her father's supervision and her last product, created without his re-modelling and cancelling. Whether the different conception of the hero is due to her father's influence or to her own altered view of life, is a question difficult to settle.

The exterior description of Lord Colambre, the hero of *The Absentee*, is limited to "a very gentleman-looking young man," [1] who had "an air of openness and generosity, a frankness, a warmth of manner, which.... irresistibly won the confidence and attracted the affection of those with whom he conversed." [2] As for his mental qualities : he was of "naturally quick and strong capacity, ardent affections, impetuous temper." [3] He was very fond of Ireland, it being his native country "endeared to him by early association and a sense of duty and patriotism," [4] but also, as he confessed himself, "because it is the country in which my father's property lies, and from which we draw our subsistence." [5] He liked his mother very much and could not endure that other people ridiculed her for her attempts at disguising her Irish descent. With his parents lived a cousin, an orphan, Grace Nugent, who had been educated by his mother and with whom he was in love.

---

[1] M. Edgeworth, *The Absentee*, Everyman's Library, p. 85.
[2] ibid., p. 127.   [3] ibid., p. 88.   [4] ibid., p. 89.   [5] ibid., p. 154.

His parents had a rich marriage in view for him, but he would not hear of it. "I have no thoughts of marrying at present and I never will marry for money." [1]) He went to Ireland to visit his father's property. Having arrived there, he was not long in making the acquaintance of Lady Dashwood, who wanted him for a husband for her daughter. These ladies happened to hear of his interest in Grace Nugent. Lady Dashwood succeeded in turning the conversation on this young lady, whom she represented as the illegitimate daughter of a relation of hers. Lord Colambre "had the greatest dread of marrying any woman whose mother had conducted herself ill. His reason, his prejudices, his pride, his delicacy, and even his limited experience, were all against it." [2]) In his despair he immediately wrote for information to his mother, who confirmed what lady Dashwood had said. Incognito he continued his journey to his father's estate, spoke with the managers, conversed with shopkeepers and cottagers and saw "to what an Irish estate and an Irish tenantry may be degraded in the absence of those whose duty and interest it is to reside in Ireland to uphold justice by example and authority; but who, neglecting this duty, commit power to bad hands and bad hearts — abandon their tenantry to oppression and their property to ruin." [3]) The scene where he disclosed himself as Lord Colambre before his father's tenants on the day that one of them wanted to have the lease of her house renewed and signed by the agent, had, according to Lord Macaulay, 'no parallel in literature since the opening of the twenty-second book of the Odyssey.' Why he travelled incognito, he explained by saying : "I was determined to see and judge how my father's estates were managed ; and I have seen, compared and judged." [4]) He was quite willing to help his father out of his financial difficulties on the condition that his parents consented to live in Ireland. When he met Miss Nugent, he was very stiff, for "to his union with her there was

---
[1]) ibid., p. 100. [2]) ibid., p. 193.
[3]) ibid., p. 242. [4]) ibid., p. 253.

an obstacle which his prudence told him ought to be unsurmountable." [1]) He decided to go into the army. However, he could not refrain from telling her — here this hero bears a striking resemblance to Miss Burney's Delville — that he was in love with her : "You see, you feel, that I love you passionately...., it is impossible that we can ever be united...., there is an invincible obstacle to our union ; of what nature I cannot explain." [2]) He left her with : "Think of me but as your cousin, your friend..." [3]) An Irish friend came to see him and persuaded him to give up his intention te enlist for the army. He spoke of a young officer he had known, who appeared to be Grace Nugent's father. It turned out, that she was a legitimate child and an heiress. Now there was no hindrance to his union with her, who understood what the 'invincible obstacle' was, but nevertheless "admired the firmness of his decision, the honour with which he had acted towards her." [4]) He returned to his native country, his beloved Ireland "happy as a lover, a friend, a son ; happy in the consciousness of having restored a father to respectability, and persuaded a mother to quit the feverish joys of fashion for the pleasure of domestic life ; happy in the hope of winning the whole heart of the woman he loved, and whose esteem, he knew, he possessed and deserved." [5])

Colambre is the moralising, didactic kind of hero. Not yet of age he is the protector of his father as well as of his mother and gets them to do what he thinks best. However, he does not bore the reader by his noble qualities and even his shrinking from taking a wife, on whose name there rests a blot, distant though this may be, does not spoil the effect that this image of Grandison makes. The authoress uses Colambre as a propagandistic hero to point out what was the cause of Ireland's growing poverty. By the mouth of her hero she pronounced the view that it must have a depressing influence on the morality of a population if the landowner is quite willing to accept high farmrents, but instead

---

[1]) ibid., p. 284.   [2]) ibid., p. 294.   [3]) ibid., p. 295.   [4]) ibid., p. 337.
[5]) ibid., p. 340.

of spending them in the country itself and making it profit by them, goes to England.

In *Helen* the novelist takes up a different point of view with regard to the hero's love for the heroine. In this novel love is the honest, sincere affection which a young man feels and keeps feeling for his once chosen idol in spite of the scandal he hears about her descent. This makes the hero more natural and attractive than lord Colambre, who forfeits the reader's admiration because he does not shrink from spoiling a girl's life only through suspicion about her descent, though he cherishes a great love for her.

Mr. Granville Beauclerc makes his appearance in the novel, when quarrelling with his uncle, who is the manager of his fortune, about a sum of money he wanted to put at the disposal of a friend. For this purpose he was quite willing "to give up his new house." [1] He was not a man who stuck to opinions, but reflected on and discussed things he was not certain about. Yet he had " 'his faggot of opinions' dragged-out and scattered about every day and each particular stick was tied and bent and twisted this way and that, and peeled and cut and hacked and unless they proved sound to the very core, not a twig of them should ever go back into his bundle." [2] This proves the seriousness of his character. The heroine liked him as "he always spoke [speaks] of women in general with respect — as if he had more confidence in them and more dependence upon them for his happiness." [3] With respect to his marriage he said: "my own will, my own heart alone must decide that matter." [4] He fell in love with Helen, who, originally an heiress, appeared to be poor at her father's death. They met at the house of a mutual friend, Lady Cecilia, who was married to General Clarendon. She rejected his proposal, having heard from lady Cecilia, that he was already secretly engaged. When she found out that she had been deceived, she wrote him a letter with explanations and

---

[1] M. Edgeworth, *Helen*, Baudrey's European Library, p. 122.
[2] ibid., p. 124.   [3] ibid., p. 271.   [4] ibid., p. 107.

accepted his suit when he returned. By some coincidence he found a bundle of love letters and her miniature, at the back of which was a dedication to her lover. Beauclerc asked Helen for an explanation, which she refused to give, being bound by a promise to lady Clarendon, the writer of the letters, and besought him to believe her without explanations.

" 'Can you trust me ?' concluded she.

'I can', cried he. 'I can — I do. By Heaven do ! I think you an angel, and legions of devils could not convince me of the contrary. I trust your word — I trust that heavenly countenance — I trust entirely....' " [1]) Instead of giving her up, he trusted her and continued to admire her greatly : "I love her a thousand times better than ever for the independence of mind she shows in thus braving my opinion, daring to set all upon the cast.... Give me a being, able to stand alone, to think and feel, decide and act, for herself." [2]) Even when the letters were talked of in the papers and general Clarendon refused to give Helen away at the altar, the hero remained her faithful lover. Yet she felt compelled to break off the engagement. In a duel he wounded his opponent dangerously and fled to the continent, having no time to state the cause of the duel. The opponent recovered and Beauclerc returned to England. Meanwhile the secret about the letters had been revealed and the noble, trusting hero led his bride in triumph to the altar.

He resembles Grandison in his good qualities, lacking, however, the arrogant self-sufficiency of this hero, whilst the sentimentality of the period is absent from him as well as from lord Colambre. In his activity, rashness and faithfulness he is a descendant of Tom Jones.

Both Miss Edgeworth's heroes stand on a far more natural plane than those of Fanny Burney, who may be considered as having founded the domestic school of novel-writing and consequently created what we may term the domestic hero. The perfection of this kind of hero the world owes to Jane Austen.

---
[1]) ibid., p. 360.   [2]) ibid., p. 360.

CHAPTER IX.

JANE AUSTEN (1775—1817).

Jane Austen is the last, but not the least of the female novelists in whose heroes relationship to Richardson's hero can be traced. She continued the method of describing the hero in society. Yet he has no longer the faultless perfection of the heroes of the other ladies, but is a being that also has his less pleasing qualities and characteristics.

Miss Austen's life was uneventful. She was the daughter of the rather well-to-do rector of Steventon in Hampshire, who was on familiar terms with the society-people of the neighbourhood. So her social experience was limited to these circles, for though she removed with her parents to Bath after her father's retirement, she kept conversing with people of the same social rank. Later on, after her father's death in 1805, she went with her mother to Southampton, where she spent four quiet years. They then removed to Chawton near Winchester where the novelist died after a lingering illness at the age of thirty-eight.

She was well-acquainted with contemporary authors and the English classics. Among her predecessors it is especially the influence of Richardson which is strongly felt. She studied his novels with great interest and appreciated them highly.

In her time Voltaire and Rousseau were eagerly read in France, so it is just possible that Jane Austen had also become acquainted with their works. Yet she does not betray this through her heroes.

Pride and Prejudice is the first novel at which she tried her hand. As it was, however, refused by publishers, it did not appear until 1813, though it was already finished in 1797. Mr. Philip Darcy, the hero, the personification of the 'Pride' of the title, was "a fine tall person with handsome features and noble mien." [1]) He was very rich, being reported as "having ten thousand a year." [2]) On the first evening of his appearance in the society of the neighbourhood he made an unpleasant impression and was pronounced to be "the proudest, most disagreeable man in the world." [3]) As for his character he was "clever," but "at the same time haughty, reserved and fastidious, and his manners though well-bred, were not inviting."[4]) How he had become so, he tells Elizabeth, when they are engaged: "I have been a selfish being all my life, in practice, though not in principle. I was given good principles.... I was spoilt by my parents, who.... allowed, encouraged, almost taught me to be selfish and overbearing — to care for none beyond my own family-circle, to think meanly of all the rest of the world.... Such I was from eight to eight and twenty." [5]) In spite of his good education and aristocratic descent, the novelist allowed her hero to speak as neither the illustrious Grandison, nor any other gentleman of Darcy's standing would have done, even in Jane Austen's time. At a ball his friend asked him to dance with a young lady, who was sitting during a waltz; looking at her he gave his opinion in these words: "tolerable, but not handsome enough to tempt me and I am in no humour at present to give consequence to young ladies who are slighted by other men." [6]) He spoke so loud that she heard all. On another occasion he preferred to be a looker-on instead of being some lady's partner; — he felt a dislike to spending an evening in such a way, because then he had "the advantage to be in vogue amongst the less polished societies of the world." [7]) Such rude behaviour contradicts Harold Child's opinion, who states that "Darcy's pride was something other than snobbishness," but "that it was

---

[1]) Jane Austen, *Pride and Prejudice*, The World's Classics, p. 7.
[2]) ibid., p. 7.   [3]) ibid., p. 7.   [4]) ibid., p. 12.   [5]) ibid., p. 319.
[6]) ibid., p. 20.   [7]) ibid., p. 20.

the result of genuinely aristocratic consciousness of merit, acting upon a haughty nature." [1]) Real aristocracy does not act in such a manner towards its fellow men. In Elizabeth Bennet, the heroine, with whom he fell in love in spite of himself he met the woman who dared contradict him and oppose his haughtiness. His pride was exhibited to the full in his proposal to her, which equalled the speech which Mortimer Delville, the hero of Fanny Burney's *Cecilia* made to the object of his admiration. "He spoke well, but there were feelings besides those of the heart to be detailed, and he was not more eloquent on the subject of tenderness than of pride. His sense of her inferiority — of its being a degradation — of the family-obstacles, which judgment had always opposed to inclination, were dwelt on with a warmth which seemed due to the consequence he was wounding, but was very unlikely to recommend his suit." [2]) The hero only expected acceptance of his proposal of marriage. Contrary to expectation he received a bold refusal and a rebuke: "had you behaved in a more gentlemanlike manner" [3]) stung him to the quick, haunted him and taught him to see that his behaviour towards Elizabeth was almost impardonable. [4]) Under his cold disdain and haughtiness, however, beat a warm, generous heart, willing to help whoever was in difficulties, as Elizabeth's sister experienced after her elopement. When they met again after eight months, "he inquired in a friendly way after her family and in all he said she heard an accent far removed from hauteur or disdain of his companions." [5]) Never before had Elizabeth seen him "so desirous to please, so free from self-consequence or unbending reserve." [6]) When after some time he asked her again to become his wife, she consented.

This is the only case in which Jane Austen tries to bring about a psychological change in her hero's character. From his height, looking down on everybody, he is brought to humiliation

---

[1]) *Cambridge History* XII, Chapter X, p. 237.
[2]) J. Austen, *Pride and Prejudice*, p. 162.
[3]) ibid., p. 317.   [4]) ibid., p. 317.   [5]) ibid., p. 223.   [6]) ibid., p. 223.

by a woman who refused to flatter his faults, but who gradually learned to see the better sides of his character, chiefly with regard to his behaviour towards her own relations. "Darcy is at first something of a caricature of dressed-up idiosyncracy and then he becomes a human being," [1]) Mr. Elton rightly observes. In his noble qualities, his readiness to help the heroine's sister and in his attitude towards Wickham, he may undoubtedly be classed among the off-spring of Richardson's hero. This statement is confirmed by Dibelius's opinion, when he says that "eine starre, schwer zu überzeugende Hartnäckigkeit stellt diesem Character ein wenig ausserhalb der Reihe Grandisons." [2]) His excessive haughtiness spoils the picture of his character; it can hardly be supposed that Jane Austen met a person among her friends whose behaviour in society corresponded with Darcy's manners. Anyhow, she applied it wrongly when she presented this haughtiness as a characteristic of persons in higher circles. Another possibility is that she gave free scope to her imagination in her wish to swerve from the regular type of hero. Lord Brabourne, Miss Austen's great-nephew, said that "he was the only one of his aunt's heroes for whom he felt regard." [3])

In Darcy the novelist created at least a man of character, who forms a strong contrast with Edward Ferrars, the hero of *Sense and Sensibility,* who has really nothing of the heroic about him; who has 'no character at all'. He was "not handsome and his manners required intimacy to make them pleasing," [4]) but "his understanding was good and his education had given it solid improvement," [5]) so that his relations hoped he would "make a fine figure in the world in some manner or other." [6]) So it was a great pity from his mother's standpoint that he had "no more talents than inclination for a public life" and that he had "no wish to be distinguished." [7]) His own wish was to enter

---

[1]) O. Elton, *A Survey of English Literature,* Vol. I, p. 194.
[2]) W. Dibelius, *Englische Romankunst,* Band II, p. 33.
[3]) Goldwin Smith, *Life of Jane Austen,* Ch. II, p. 78.
[4]) J. Austen, *Sense and Sensibility,* Tauchnitz e.d., p. 14.
[5]) ibid., p. 14.   [6]) ibid., p. 14.   [7]) ibid., p. 69.

the Church, but in this he was baulked by his mother, on whom he was financially dependent, who thought a position in the Church not one that could add more glory to their name. So he gave up his intention, because he lacked independence, which people attributed to his "want of spirits, of openness and of consistency." [1] He fell in love with Lucy Steel, a girl of the lower classes, a choice which his mother again could not approve of. The result was that she cut him off entirely on hearing of their secret engagement. Lucy then broke off their betrothal. Soon after he felt that unknowingly he had been in love with Ellinor, the girl whom his mother had educated with her own children. He proposed to her and was accepted. The better side of his character then manifested itself, for he refused to ask his mother's pardon in a letter of submission, or her assistance in helping him out of his pecuniary difficulties. "I can make no submission — I am grown neither humble nor penitent by what has passed. I am grown very happy, but that would not interest. I know of no submission that is proper for me to make." [2] He carried out his original intention to enter the Church and succeeded in providing for himself and his wife.

He is a very weak example of the Grandison-type, if any example at all. In his fortnight's absence without anybody's knowing his whereabouts, and in his keeping his betrothal to Lucy Steel a secret for four years, he reveals characteristics of Tom Jones or of the picaresque hero. For the rest, he is a docile, meek kind of person. Dibelius states: "Edward Ferrars mangelhafte Erziehung und das Fehlen jedes ernsteren Lebensberuf haben ihn unglücklich und schwankend gemacht." [3] When his love, however, forces him to shift for himself he sticks to his former decision to enter upon the profession which is most in keeping with his character. Taking all his deeds into consideration, he is after all an inferior hero, in whom it is difficult to see 'the immaculate gentleman.' Nor can one side with

---

[1] ibid., p. 77.   [2] ibid., p. 279.
[3] W. Dibelius, *Englische Romankunst*, Band II, p. 75.

Dibelius, who classes him among the imitations of Grandison.

An important improvement upon this character is the hero of *Mansfield Park*. Edmund Bertram was the same kind, indulgent sort of person, who also felt attracted to the Church, but who is at least a man "with strong good sense and uprightness of mind." [1]) He was "der Mensch mit dem feinen Verständniss für inneren Menschenwert, dem zurückhaltende Takt und der Freude am Wohltun," [2]) a statement which is confirmed by his behaviour towards his cousin Fanny, whose constant protector he had remained from the moment he found her on the staircase crying for her mother. "Edmund's friendship never failed her : his leaving Eton for Oxford made no change in his kind disposition.... he was always true to her interests, and considerate to her feelings,.... giving her advice, consolation, and encouragement." [3]) Like Edward Ferrars he fell in love with an unworthy creature who first encouraged him, looking upon him as the future head of the family. Hearing that he was "to be a clergyman," [4]) she made no further attempts at attracting him. In his love he resembled the sentimental hero and spoke of the girl he loved to his confidante Fanny, as "the only woman in the world whom [he] could ever think of as his wife." [5]) The following quotation proves the nobility of his character and his respect for the profession he had chosen : "I could better bear to lose her (the woman he is in love with), because not rich enough, than because of my profession. That would only prove her affection not equal to sacrifices." [6]) A certain unsteadiness of character was revealed in him when he was persuaded to take part in a theatrical performance which he at first absolutely refused as not being in keeping with the character of a future clergyman. He gave in at last, because he was the only suitable person to be found who could play the part of a clergyman and so "Edmund had descended from that moral elevation which

---

[1]) Jane Austen, *Mansfield Park*, Everyman's Library, p. 16.
[2]) W. Dibelius, Englische Romankunst, Band II, p. 73.
[3]) Jane Austen, Mansfield Park, p. 17.
[4]) ibid., p. 16.   [5]) ibid., p. 351.   [6]) ibid., p. 352.

he had maintained before. [1]) When a series of misfortunes fell upon his family, his presence was necessary at home. He was staying with the same family as Fanny, whom he pressed to his heart when the news was told to him saying "with only these words, just articulate : 'My Fanny, my only sister, my only comfort now'." [2]) When they travelled home together "he looked very ill ; evidently suffering under violent emotions" [3]) and "his deep sighs often reached [her]." [3])

The old sentimentality is again conspicuous here. This man, who is the only being the whole family, especially Sir Thomas Bertram, looks up to for support and help in their difficulties, is rather weak by betraying and not by controlling his emotions.

Later on he told Fanny of his own disappointment in the girl whom he wanted for his wife. But in course of time [I purposely obstain from dates on this occasion, says Miss Austen], [4]) he got over his disappointment and "became anxious to marry Fanny." [5])

Edmund Bertram resembles Sir Charles Grandison most of all Miss Austen's heroes, having all his good characteristics, but still being a prig. She tries to make him more natural by suffering him to be persuaded to take part in the dramatic performance, which, though not a serious fault of character, still diminishes the pleasant impression already made upon the reader. Moreover he is for a young man too exaggerated in the choice of his words to express his emotions.

Mr. Knightley, the hero of her last novel *Emma* is the picture of the country-gentleman. He is the character that is not blasted by any fault or weak moment ; yet he does not bore the reader by his perfection. He was "a sensible man about seven or eight and thirty," [6]) with "a tall, firm, upright figure" [7]) and "a great deal of health, activity and independence." [8]) He had "a downright,

---

[1]) ibid., p. 131.   [2]) ibid., p. 372.   [3]) ibid., p. 372.   [4]) ibid., p. 393.
[5]) ibid., p. 393.
[6]) J. Austen, *Emma*, The World's Classics, p. 5.
[7]) ibid., p. 304.   [8]) ibid., p. 197.

decided, commanding sort of manner about him" which "his figure and look and his situation in life seemed to allow." [1]) To the heroine's fussy, tiresome father he was very indulgent, and always willing to talk with him and listen to his endless stories. He had known the heroine from her youth, and was "one of the few people who could see faults in Emma Woodhouse, and the only one who ever told her of them." [2]) He was highly indignant at her interfering in other people's love-affairs, and when she was very rude to an old lady-friend of theirs, Miss Bates, he told her straight-out how unlike a lady she had behaved : "This is not pleasant to you, Emma, and it is very far from pleasant to me ; but I must, I will — I will tell you truths while I can, satisfied with proving myself your friend by very faithful counsel, and trusting that you will some time or other do me greater justice than you can do now." [3]) Unknowingly he was in love with Emma, whom "from family attachment and habit, and thorough excellence of mind, he had loved, and watched over from a girl, with an endeavour to improve her" ; [4]) yet he had never thought of a marriage with her, considering himself too old. When Frank Churchill appeared and Knightley saw the apparent love between the two, he knew that he loved her. Frank was in love with somebody else, and Emma said that she had never thought of Frank as her future husband. Then he could not control himself any longer and betrayed his love for her. Though "he had blamed and lectured her" [5]) he was accepted as her betrothed.

Mr. Knightley is the best of the heroes for his constancy of character ; he is "the natural supplement of [the heroine], the corrective of her faults and the support to which her charming weakness clings." [6]) He never wavers from his determination to be her champion and would have sacrificed his own hopes if she had met with a man worthy of becoming her husband. Dibelius sees in this character the general characteristics of Grandison,

---

[1]) ibid., p. 29.   [2]) ibid., p. 7.   [3]) ibid., p. 353.   [4]) ibid., p. 391.
[5]) ibid., p. 406.
[6]) Goldwin Smith. *Life of Jane Austen*, Ch. IX, p. 189.

"aber mit besonderer Betonung des klaren Blicks und des ernsten Rechtgefühles." [1])

All Jane Austen's heroes have a foundation of reality, to which qualities of Richardson's hero are added. However, they lack this prototype's self-sufficiency and conceitedness. While Sir Charles Grandison was created with a moral and didactic purpose, it was never Miss Austen's intention to write "unto intellectual and moral edification." [2]) She pictures her first and her third hero with a blot on his character to increase his naturalness and to remove the impression of perfection. However, she makes the fourth too old and too seriousminded to be the hero of a girl of about twenty, which opinion is also held by Jane Austen's nephew, Lord Brabourne.

Charlotte Brontë wrote to Mr. Williams her opinion respecting Jane Austen's characters and her statement is right in so far as it is applicable to her heroes : "....The passions are unknown to her. Her business is not half so much with the human heart as with the human eye.... What throbs fast and full, though hidden, what the blood rushes through, what is the unseen seat of life and the sentient target of death, this Miss Austen ignores...." [3]) Leonie Villard is right when she observes : "Le caractère masculin n'est jamais observé d'une façon bien profonde ; cependant, cette étude est précieuse puisqu'elle nous indique, à défaut de ce que sont les hommes, comment ils apparaissent aux yeux des femmes," [4]) whilst Mr. Léon Boucher states his opinion more eloquently in these words : "Jamais elle ne se trahit derrière eux ; elle les laisse agir et parler sans se mêler à leurs actes ou à leur conversation, abandonnant au lecteur intelligent le plaisir de les comprendre et le soin de les juger. C'est à leur allure qu'on les reconnaît." [5])

Nothing is revealed through her heroes concerning her religious

---

[1] W. Dibelius, *Englische Romankunst*, Band II, p. 73.
[2] Harold Williams, *Modern English Writers*, p. 275.
[3] Letter from Ch. Brontë to W. S. Williams, April 12 th, 1850.
[4] Leonie Villard, *Jane Austen, sa Vie et son Oeuvre*, Bk. II, Ch. II, p. 246.
[5] *Revue des Deux Mondes*, 15 Sept., 1878.

feelings, her political or humanitarian views, or her opinions on the leading questions of the period in which she lived. Mr. Goldwin Smith says : "Her heroes betray no vestige of any of the revolutionary or anti-revolutionary writers, who dealt with the great intellectual movements of the age, no trace of philosophic or scientific study." [1]) Only Darcy, the hero of her first novel, shows a slight attempt at character development.

The novelist only pictured her hero in his attitude towards the heroine as a future husband and he shows his feelings "by attentions, by proposals, by manner, by anything except passion." [2]) His character is revealed through his deeds, but the background of these deeds, the motives or causes that led to them, is hidden from the reader, because Miss Austen "never penetrated into the deeper experiences, the powerful, emotional and spiritual things of life." [3]) That is why Legious and Cazamian are absolutely wrong when they say that "her clear-sighted eyes read through the inner minds of those who lived around her or of the beings whom she invents and animates." [4]) Her heroes distinctly betray lack of personal experience, and she succeeded in supplying what was wanting partly by intuition, but for the greater part by imitation of what her predecessors, chiefly Richardson, had already produced. She was well aware of her limited experience, for when Mr. Clarke, the librarian of Carlton House in 1815 asked her to describe the life of a clergyman who should spend his time between the metropolis and the country, she wrote back : "I am quite honoured by your thinking me capable of drawing such a clergyman as you gave the sketch of in your note of Nov. 16. But I assure you I am not. The comic part of the character I might be equal to, but not the good, the enthusiastic, the literary. Such a man's conversation must at times be on subjects of science and philosophy, of which I know

---

[1]) Goldwin Smith, *Life of Jane Austen*, Ch. I, p. 23.
[2]) O. Elton, *A Survey of English literature*, p. 199.
[3]) Statement of G. Eliot, found in W. H. Hudson, Introduction into the Study of Literature, p. 176.
[4]) Legouis and Cazamian, *A History of English Literature*, Vol. II, p. 243.

nothing. A classical education, or at any rate a very extensive acquaintance with English literature, ancient and modern, appears to me quite indispensable for the person who would do any justice to your clergyman." [1])

She also declined to write a historical romance illustrative of the august House of Coburg, for the same reason, openly avowing: "I could not sit down to write a serious romance under any other motive than to save my life ; ....I must keep to my own style and go on in my own way ; and though I may never succeed again in that, I am convinced that I should totally fail in any other." [2])

Jane Austen, like the other novelists discussed, lived in a time when the general mind was occupied with the troubles caused by the French revolution and French supremacay and oppression throughout Europe. They did not and could not think of what lesson this period had to teach, nor do thoughts on problems of a spiritual nature occupy them. This is reserved for a later generation, which had to face the industrial troubles that followed the French wars and the subsequent rise of democracy. Then man is no longer seen as a being by himself, but is considered as "a spirit bound by invisible bonds to all Men." [3]) Before we shall treat the authoresses who wanted to improve the condition of man and to come to a better understanding of the link between man and his fellow-creatures, two further novelists claim our attention. These surprised the world with heroes entirely different from the current type. They are Charlotte Brontë and her sister Emily.

---

[1]) Preface to *Emma,* The World's Classic edition.
[2]) ibid.
[3]) Th. Carlyle, *Sartor Resartus,* Collins Classics, p. 57.

CHAPTER X.

CHARLOTTE BRONTË (1816—1855).

Nearly forty years elapsed between the publication of Jane Austen's last novel and the announcement of Charlotte Brontë's first. This period was one of transition. Romanticism had celebrated its greatest triumphs, and a longing for reality had set in : "after the rule of emotions, dreams and the tumults of the soul, there came [comes] a time when the need of an order born of reason began [begins] to manifest itself." [1] It was a time of great importance for the industrial world ; the practical application of steam to factories and means of conveyance, the consequent growth of the manufactory system led to enormous activity and great mental energy.

In the field of literature romanticism continued to exercise its influence for some time, however, till through Dickens the new spirit of realism, a natural consequence of the industrial activity, found its expression in the novel. The reading public could no longer be confronted with a hero of a bygone past or with a picture of perfection, which borders on unreality ; it wanted a natural being for its hero, placed in an environment of its own time.

Dickens took his heroes from the middle and lower classes. He sought to point out some existing abuse and to rouse sympathy and interest for its reform through the descriptions of the hardships and privations to which the heroes had been subjected.

The other author who broke with the traditional hero was the

---

[1] Legouis and Cazamian, *A History of English Literature,* Vol. II, Bk. VI, p. 323.

caricaturist Thackeray, who liked to observe the follies and peculiarities of people and took for his heroes apparently unidealistic figures, who became attractive and interesting through his vision of them. Before Thackeray published his first real novel, a woman appeared in the field of English letters who has described a hero whose career was entirely true to real life, and whose character not only manifested its good qualities, but was also endowed with faults and vices.

It is not *La vie de Charlotte Brontë* par Mrs. Gaskell as Mr. Emile Montégut observes, but Charlotte Brontë herself, who "marque une transition, non seulement entre deux générations différentes, mais entre deux états de société et deux manières de sentir et de penser." [1]) These words reflect Professor Saintsbury's opinion when he says : "her work stands in the middle of the century, obviously transitional, distinguished as much from Thackeray and from Dickens by a curious spirit of irregular and stunted romanticism, as from the romantics proper by a realist touch no less unmistakable." [2]) This fact must necessarily be revealed in the conception of her heroes who are men absolutely different from the monotonous perfections, "the pink of kindness and graciousness" [3]) which the women at the end of the eighteenth century issued into the world.

"The Brontës belong to a class of writers whom it is impossible to understand except through the medium of biography," [4]) says Hugh Walter, who is not alone in his opinion. In the limited space which can be reserved for the description of the chief events of their lives it would be impossible to picture the dull, dreary, maddening monotony of the sisters' existence. It is owing to their living far from any cultured and intellectual intercourse, the dullness of their parental home, their lack of courage or too great filial devotion that prevented them from breaking the bonds which

---

[1]) E. Montégut, *Ecrivains modernes de l'Angleterre*, Portrait général, p. 183.
[2]) G. Saintsbury, *A short History of English Literature*, p. 748.
[3]) W. L. Cross, *Development of the English Novel*, p. 227.
[4]) H. Walker, *The Literature of the Victorian Era*, Ch. III, p. 710.

bound them. Mrs. Humphry Ward expressed the impression made on her by the sisters Brontë in a sonnet, the opening lines of which reflect so strikingly their characters and their surroundings:

> Pale Sisters! reared amid the purple sea
> Of windy moorland, where, remote, ye plied
> All houschold arts, meek, passion-taught, and free,
> Kinship your joy, and Fantasy your guide! — [1])

Charlotte Brontë was born on June 29th 1816 and was the eldest daughter of the Reverend Patrick Brontë, minister of Haworth at that time. Her mother died when she was young. Her father gave her elementary instruction, and, when fifteen years old, she was sent to the boarding-school at Roehead, where she afterwards became a teacher. In this profession she did not succeed very well; she left the school and became a governess in a private family. With her two sisters she formed a plan to establish a school of their own. In order to learn foreign languages she went to Brussels, and, at the age of twenty-six became a pupil at a boarding-school, the headmaster of which was to take such an important place in her life. Afterwards she became a teacher of English in this school. After the death of her aunt who managed her father's household, she had to come home. From this time began the monotonous life that ended in her death in the thirty-ninth year of her life, after a short but happy marriage to Mr. Nicholls, her father's curate. She had seen all her sisters and only brother go before her.

From her childhood she had lived at Haworth in Yorkshire, a very remote district. In winter it was mostly isolated by the snow. The population was sturdy, self-reliant, harsh and money-loving. "These men are keen and shrewd; faithful and persevering in following out a good purpose, fell in tracking an evil one. They are not emotional; they are not easily made into either friends or enemies, but once lovers or haters, it is difficult to

---

[1]) *Cornhill Magazine*, Febr., 1900.

change their feeling ; they are a powerful race both in mind and body, both for good and evil," [1]) says Mrs. Gaskell. Such was the population by which Charlotte Brontë and her sisters were surrounded after their coming home from Brussels. She herself writes : "Education had made little progress among them, there was no inducement to seek social intercourse beyond our own domestic circle, we were wholly dependent on ourselves and each other, on books and study, for the enjoyments and occupations of life. The highest stimulus, as well as the liveliest pleasure we had known from childhood upwards, lay in attempts at literary composition.... We had early cherished the dream of one day becoming authors." [2]) To escape the dullness of their existence Charlotte and her two sisters started novel-writing. At that time "her taste and judgment had revolted against the exaggerated idealisms of her early girlhood, and she went to the extreme of reality, closely depicting characters as they had shown themselves to her in actual life ; if they were strong even to coarseness, — as was the case with some that she had met with in flesh and blood existence, — she 'wrote them down an ass' " [3]) her biographer states.

Her conception of her hero Charlotte gave in the preface to *The Professor :* "my hero should work his way through life as I had seen real living men work theirs — that he should never get a shilling he had not earned — that not sudden turns should lift him in a moment to wealth and high station; that whatever small competency he might gain, should be won by the sweat of his brow ; that, before he could find so much as an arbour to sit down, he should master at least half the ascent of 'the Hill of Difficulty', that he should not even marry a beautiful girl or a lady of rank. As Adam's son he should share Adam's doom, and drain throughout life a mixed and moderate cup of enjoyment."

She really made her first hero, William Crimsworth, spend

---

[1]) Mrs. E. C. Gaskell, *The Life of Charlotte Brontë,* p. 8.
[2]) Biographical note of Ellis and Acton Bell in *Wuthering Heights,* by Currer Bell.
[3]) E. C. Gaskell, *The Life of Charlotte Brontë,* p. 212.

a life of struggle. He was a man with "a thin irregular face ; sunk, dark eyes under a large square forehead ; complexion destitute of bloom and attraction, something young, but not youthful." [1]) He worked some time at his brother's cottonmill. This brother, however, treated him like the lowest clerk. Though he found himself disappointed in his situation, he said : "I would have endured in silence the rust and cramp of my best faculties."[2]) Through the mediation of one of his brother's friends he became a teacher at a Brussels boarding-school, where "in a few weeks [he] conquered the teasing difficulties inseparable from the commencement of almost every career." [3]) He was also invited to give lessons at Mlle. Reuter's girls' school where one morning a new pupil appeared, a young, slight girl, very plain and shy. In the following lines the authoress reveals the harsh self-reliant character of the Yorkshire race in the manner in which the hero tried to make the girl self-reliant. He saw clearly that she could not follow and note down his dictations, but he did not help her, on the contrary "dictated a little faster."[4]) His manner of adressing her was always peremptory as he considered a tone of command "the only way with diffident easily embarrassed characters." [5]) He soon found out the best way to treat this girl : "constancy of attention — a kindness as mute as watchful, always standing by her, cloaked in the rough garb of austerity, and making its real nature known only by a rare glance of interest, or a cordial and gentle word ; real respect masked with seeming imperiousness, directing, urging her actions, yet helping her too, and that with devoted care." [6]) His feeling of honour and righteousness forced him to give up his position at the girls' school, because Miss Reuter, who was "at least ten years older than he," [7]) had fallen in love with him, which love he could not return. Later on he found out what the character was of Mr. Pelet, his headmaster, with whom he had always been on

---

[1]) Currer Bell, *The Professor,* Tauchnitz ed., p. 97.
[2]) ibid., p. 34.   [3]) ibid., p. 84.   [4]) ibid., p. 163.   [5]) ibid., p. 179.
[6]) ibid., p. 197.   [7]) ibid., p. 144.

friendly terms. Then he resigned from this school also. The reason he stated in the following terms: "once convinced that my friend's disposition is incompatible with my own, once assured that he is indelibly stained with certain defects obnoxious to my principles, I dissolve the connection." [1]) He had no situation now and wanted to marry, having fallen in love with his shy pupil. "His stubborn monitor 'conscience' had said: "Do what you feel is right; obey me and even in the sloughs of want I will plant for you firm footing." [2]) Then rose upon him — Ch. Brontë betrays her unwavering faith and trust in God here — "a strange, inly-felt idea of some Great Being, unseen, but all present, who, in his beneficence, desired only my welfare.... waited to see wether I should obey his voice." [3]) He succeeded in getting a new situation, and was married to Frances, who was good and dear to him because "he was to her a good, just and faithful husband." [4])

This novel is an immature composition. Its hero was drawn from Mr. Héger, the headmaster of the Brussels boardingschool, where Charlotte was a pupil. The connection between the two is, however, only to be traced in their outward appearance and their domineering way of speaking. The hero with his conceit and high opinion of himself, who is "not a character, but a stick," [5]) has nothing in common with the powerful, choleric and irritable example, who was "a genuine force of character, something of the genius of exposition and a touch of that irony or semi-humorous malice, which is the salt of personality." [6])

Mr. Héger is also to be found in Charlotte's last novel, but is then the active, vehement little headmaster. The two other heroes, Rochester and Moore are, as Mrs. Gaskell suspects, pictures of the many-sided sons of the family of Yorke, with whom the Brontës were well-acquainted. "From these" she says, "she drew all that there was of truth in the character of the heroes of her

---

[1]) ibid., p. 147.   [2]) ibid., p. 253.   [3]) ibid., p. 253.   [4]) ibid., p. 342.
[5]) J. A. Falconer, *The Professor and Villette,* Engl. Studies, April, 1927.
[6]) *Cambridge History* XIII, p. 405.

first two works." [1]) These two heroes have inherent in them many qualities of the West-Yorkshire character; a mixture of the Anglo-Saxon and the Norseman.

Rochester found his ancestor in the adventurous hero; he had travelled all over the world, did not feel very much at home at his own Hall, and when he had spent a short time there, invariably set out on new journeys. He was a muscular man of about "thirty-five," [2]) "of the middle height, with black hair, a colourless, olive face, a square massive brow, broad and jetty eyebrows, a decisive nose, a firm, grim mouth [3]) and great, dark eyes. [4]) His housekeeper spoke of him with great respect. Adèle was fond of her father. Rochester's behaviour towards the young governess, when she was presented to him, did not make a pleasant impression on her. He soon began to tell her of his former life, at which self-revelation he was himself surprised for he said to her one day: "Strange that I should choose you for the confidante of all this, young lady; ....as if it were the most usual thing in the world for a man like me to tell stories of his opera-mistresses to a quaint, inexperienced girl like you." [5]) "When I was as old as you, I was a feeling fellow enough; partial to the unfledged, unfostered, and unlucky; but Fortune.... has kneaded me with her knuckles and now I flatter myself I am hard and tough as an India-rubber ball." [6]) "Nature meant me to be, on the whole, a good man...." "When fate wronged me,.... I turned desperate; then I degenerated" [7]) he continued after he had confessed: "I have a past existence, a series of deeds, a colour of life to contemplate within my own breast, which might well call my sneers and censures from my neighbours to myself." [8]) He even told her of Adèle's birth and his relation to her mother, which betrays little delicacy of character,

---

[1]) E. C. Gaskell, *The Life of Ch. Brontë*, 277. [As *The Professor* was published after Charlotte Brontë's death, Mrs. Gaskell means by the first two works: *Jane Eyre* and *Shirley*.]
[2]) Ch. Brontë, *Jane Eyre*, Collins' ed., p. 125.
[3]) ibid., p. 190.   [4]) ibid., p. 143.
[5]) ibid., p. 157.   [6]) ibid., p. 145.   [7]) ibid., p. 149.   [8]) ibid., p. 148.

considering he was speaking to a girl not yet out of her teens. In various ways — first disguised as a fortuneteller, later on pretending he was going to be married — he tried to find out if she was in love with him, and when at last he was sure of it, he proposed to her and was accepted in spite of the fact, that he was often "proud, sardonic, harsh to inferiority of every description" [1] and that she knew that "his great kindness to [her] was balanced by unjust severity to many others." [2] On the wedding-morning he looked "bent up to a purpose" and "grimly resolute." [3] When the minister had asked, if there was any impediment to the marriage, a man came forward to say there was, to which Rochester's brother-in-law, Mason, bore evidence. Then "his eye had a tawny, nay, a bloody light in its gloom." [4] He would have knocked this man down, but fortunately controlled himself in time and explained his behaviour to the bystanders: "I meant to be a bigamist; but fate has out-manoeuvred me, or Providence has checked me — perhaps the last. I am little better than a devil at this moment." [5] He acknowledged that he was married, but that his wife was insane and invited the people present to accompany him to see for themselves. When they were in the lunatic's room, his wife nearly throttled him. The next day he apologized to Jane, the heroine, by saying that "he never meant to wound her thus" [6] and "there was such deep remorse in his eye, such true pity in his tone, such manly energy in his manner: and besides, there was such unchanged love in his whole look and mien" [7] that the heroine forgave him at once. He told her the whole story of his unhappy marriage into which he had been ensnared, of his wife's madness and how he had locked her up at his Hall, since when he had wandered all over the world to find a woman he could love, and now had found in Jane. Being afraid that she would refuse him, if she knew of his first marriage, he had kept it a secret from her. In spite of his vehement expressions of repentance [e. g.

---

[1]) ibid., p. 161.   [2]) ibid., p. 161.   [3]) ibid., p. 313.   [4]) ibid., p. 316.
[5]) ibid., p. 317.   [6]) ibid., p. 324.   [7]) ibid., p. 324.

"if the man who had but one little ewe-lamb that was dear to him as a daughter,.... had by some mistake slaughtered it at the shambles, he would not have rued his bloody blunder more than I now rue mine" ¹)] he tried to persuade her to live with him, but she refused. Jane left the house and found another situation. The lunatic wife set the house on fire ; Rochester in trying to save her lost his eyesight and his left arm. When Jane heard this she returned to him and married him. By this time he had begun "to see and acknowledge the hand of God in his [my] doom, to experience remorse, repentance, the wish for reconcilement to his [my] Maker." ²)

As *The Professor* was not accepted by any of the publishers, Charlotte Brontë found out that these men did not like lifelike description, but preferred "something more imaginative and poetical." ³)

In creating Rochester, it was the novelist's purpose to represent him as a man, who has "a thoughtful nature and a very feeling heart ; he is neither selfish nor self-indulgent, he is ill-educated, misguided, errs, when he does err, through rashness and inexperience ; he lives for a time as too many men live, but being radically better than most men, he does not like the degraded life, and is never happy in it. He is taught the severe lessons of experience and has sense to learn wisdom from them. Years improve him, the effervescence of youth foamed away, what is really good in him still remains. His nature is like wine of a good vintage : time cannot sour, but only mellows him." ⁴)

She depicted in reality an abnormally self-centred man, strong as regards muscles and frame ; but the reader never becomes acquainted with anything great and powerful in his actions calling forth admiration. The one deed he performs is one which is abhorrent to the general reader. "The attempt to entrap Jane into a bigamous connection by concealing his wife's existence

---

[1] ibid., p. 324.   [2] ibid., p. 486.
[3] Preface to *The Professor*.
[4] Letter from Ch. Brontë to W. S. Williams, Aug. 14th, 1848.

is a piece of treachery for which it is hard to forgive him," [1] Leslie Stephen rightly remarks. He imposes upon a girl fresh from school and without any worldly experience ; by telling her of the failure of his life he made an appeal to her sympathy and her generous self-sacrifice. In this conduct he is a man "who would have been the villain in the old novel." [2] He is often supposed to represent the average man of the authoress's immediate surroundings. She knew these domineering characters, she had experienced the tyranny of her egotistic father and her degraded brother ; she knew, most likely from personal experience that harshness and domineering can have the effect on shy, diffident women to call forth their energy and to give them boldness to speak and act for themselves. She spoils this portrait of partly observation, but formed for the greater part in her imagination, by adding the story of the hero's intended bigamy. This deed of simply ignoring his legal wife's existence turns him into an inferior being. Leslie Stephen called him "a knave to entrap a defenceless girl by a mock ceremony." [3] It is impossible to see the tenability of Mr. A. Swinburne's assertion that Rochester is one of "the only two male figures of wholly truthful workmanship and vitally heroic mould ever carved and coloured by woman's hand." [4] The authoress puts in him the fire that is burning within herself when he seeks to break the bonds that keep him from starting a new life, a life that in Rochester would call forth all his energies and find its satisfaction in the love of a sympathetic spouse. He is hampered by his insane wife, whilst the authoress is constantly kept from breaking away from her surroundings by her sense of duty towards her relations.

Rochester also represents the unsatisfied longing slumbering in the inmost recesses of Charlotte's heart. In this hero the present writer found for the first time what she vainly expected to find in all the heroes, though not in the same degree: something

---

[1] L. Stephen, *Hours in a Library,* Vol. III, p. 24.
[2] W. L. Cross, *Development of the English Novel,* p. 229.
[3] L. Stephen, Hours in a Library, Vol. III, p. 24.
[4] A. C. Swinburne, *A Note on Charlotte Brontë,* p. 27.

of the novelist's own secret ideal. So Prof. Saintsbury is quite right when he says that there seems to be "a certain projection of the ideal," though "the ideal was a rather poor one. It was as much of a schoolgirl's or a governess's hero as any one of Scott's and Byron's." [1])

Contemporary critics did not judge this novel very favourably. *The North British Review* of 1849 declared: " if Jane Eyre be the production of a woman, she must be a woman unsexed." Another critic was of opinion that the authoress must be one who for some sufficient reason had long forfeited the society of her own sex, [2]) whilst the *Economist* pronounced it 'odious, if the work of a woman'.

Mr. G. H. Lewes, the critic of *Fraser's Magazine* was the man who saw the failure of this hero and the cause of it and wrote to the authoress "not to stray from the ground of experience, as she became weak, when she entered the reign of fiction." In her answer she put the question: Is not the experience of each individual limited, and ought one "to be deaf to the demands of imagination which was a strong, restless faculty, which claims to be heard and exercised ?" [3])

As it is hardly possible that Charlotte Brontë created the last part of her hero's life from observation, it seems more likely that she imitated it, as is supposed, after a tale of Sheridan Le Fanu, published in the *Dublin University Magazine* in 1839.

In her next novel she returns again to reality with only occasional touches of imagination.

The hero of *Shirley*, Robert Moore, is the true representative of the harsh, but energetic employers, one of the thousands, on whom the starving poor of Yorkshire seemed to have a closer claim. It is supposed that she created her hero after reading a story that was afloat then, to which supposition the hero's descent from an English father and a French mother might have

---

[1]) G. Saintsbury, *Three Mid-Century Novelists*, p. 278.
[2]) *Quaterly Review*, Dec., 1848.
[3]) Letter from Ch. Brontë to G. H. Lewes, Esq. Nov. 6th, 1847.

given rise. H. Walker remarks that he is, "even in such a trifle as his half-foreign blood, identical with the Cartwright who was the real hero of the Luddite story, which first set her imagination to work." [1]) Robert Moore was a strange-looking man, thin, dark and sallow, very foreign in aspect [2]) with large, grave, and grey eyes, [3]) of about thirty years of age and of a foreign ancestry by the mother's side.[4]) It was his aim to restore the large fortune which his forefathers once possessed, but which was partly lost by speculations, and totally by the French revolution. His aim had made him selfish, and he did not care if the introduction of new machines "threw the old workman out of employ." [5]) Harshness and egoism, the dominant traits of the North-English character, were his main characteristics, which Caronline Helstone, who loved him, hoped to improve by pointing them out to him. When they were reading Shakespeare's *Corolianus* she remarked: "You sympathize with that proud patrician who does not sympathize with his famished fellow-men, and insults them." [6]) He asked her why Corolianus was hated by the citizens, to which she answered : ".... you must not be proud to your workpeople; you must not neglect chances of soothing them, and you must not be of an inflexible nature, uttering a request as austerely as if it were a command." [7]) When the twelve deputees of the working-people came to ask him "to make changes more slowly," [8]) he answered the spokesman very abruptly that he should have his own way and that if they broke the machines, he should still get others, winding up with these words: "I'll never give in." [9]) The man to whom this answer was addressed, was an honest fellow, quite willing to work. Though he spoke these unkind words, Moore's better nature asserted itself, and he persuaded a friend to take the man into his service. He could not help him himself, because his affairs were in such a state that "he didn't

---

[1]) H. Walker, *The Literature of the Victorian Era*, p. 718.
[2]) Ch. Brontë, *Shirley*, Caxton-novels ed., p. 8.
[3]) ibid., p. 9.   [4]) ibid., p. 9.   [5]) ibid., p. 9.   [6]) ibid., p. 30.
[7]) ibid., p. 31.   [8]) ibid., p. 46.   [9]) ibid., p. 46.

know where to turn...." [1]) His friend advised him to look for a rich wife. The discontented labourers attacked his mill, but he was prepared, and "stood the defence with unflinching firmness." [2]) The rioters disappeared; he did not pursue" the mob, the mere followers," but the leaders "he hunted like any sleuthhound; and well he liked the occupation: its excitement was of a kind pleasant to his nature; he liked it better than cloth-making." [3]) This is a typical trait of the Yorkshire character to which Ch. Brontë draws attention. Moore was not satisfied with detecting the leaders but "had attended their trial, heard their conviction and sentence and seen them safely shipped prior to transportation." [4]) He knew that the workmen would attack his works again, but he was not afraid, being "too proud — too hard-natured — too phlegmatic a man to fear." [5]) At last he followed his friend's advice and proposed to a rich heiress, who, knowing that he was not in love with her, rejected his proposal. He was attacked by friends of the workmen whose deportation he had promoted, and was knocked down. He was taken to his friend's house and nursed. Here Caroline visited him secretly, and to her he told his affair with the rich heiress saying: "I suppose I was truly tempted by the mere gilding of the bait." [6]) After some time he asked Caroline to become his wife and was accepted as her future husband.

Ch. Brontë succeeded in placing before the reader the portrait of a man, who bears the striking features of the male population of her district — the then average manufacturer — of one of those people who cared for nobody and nothing except their mill and who justified every measure, fair or foul, if it were necessary for the maintenance of it. A similar hero is described in *North and South* by Mrs. Gaskell, but whether the authoresses, who where friends and discussed their writings together. borrowed from each other is a question difficult to settle.

The hero of her last novel is the other one of the two male

---

[1]) ibid., p. 55. [2]) ibid., p. 116. [3]) ibid., p. 129. [4]) ibid., p. 176.
[5]) ibid., p. 129. [6]) ibid., p. 202.

figures which Mr. Swinburne admired so much. Paul Emanuel, the little man with "his close-shorn black head,[1]) black whiskers and blue eyes,[2]) a brow marked and square,[3]) a nose with wide quivering nostrils[4]) and a swart, sallow darkness of complexion, which spoke his Spanish blood,[5]) was a careful reproduction of her Brussels headmaster. He was "very irritable, which one could hear when he apostrophised with vehemence the awkward squad under his orders"[6]) and was sure "to revolt against what was urgent and obligatory."[7]) Further he carried on "a constant crusade against" the 'amour propre' of every human being but himself,"[8]) but also knew how to compel his pupils "to demean themselves with heroism and self-possession."[9]) He was all fury "when his questioning eyes met dishonest denial of some wrong,"[10]) yet he could "pity and forgive if it were acknowledged candidly."[11]) Upon the heroine he exercised the same method of keeping her down, as the hero in *The Professor*, a method which must have made a deep impression on Charlotte's shy nature and have made her realize its efficacy. When the heroine was helpless and could not go on with her work, he was "very kind, very good, very forbearing, because he felt the weighty humiliation imposed by his own sense of incapacity."[12]) As soon as she had mastered the difficulties "his kindness became sternness; he fretted, he opposed, he curbed [her] imperiously."[13]) But the heroine confessed that when he sneered at her, "....his injustice stirred in her [me] ambitious wishes... it gave wings to aspiration."[14]) He was once in love with a girl, but was thwarted by her grandmother. His fiancée retired to a convent and died there. When the same grandmother was in financial difficulties later on, he helped her because he felt he owed this to his deceased betrothed, but was forced by this to live very economically. He offered the heroine his friendship which "was a support

---

[1]) Ch. Brontë, *Villette*, The World's Cassics, p. 144.
[2]) ibid., p. 175. [3]) ibid., p. 390. [4]) ibid., p. 144. [5]) ibid., p. 371.
[6]) ibid., p. 144. [7]) ibid., p. 374. [8]) ibid., p. 174. [9]) ibid., p. 247.
[10]) ibid., p. 388. [11]) ibid., p. 388. [12]) ibid., p. 406. [13]) ibid., p. 406.
[14]) ibid., p. 406.

like that of some rock." [1]) Being a Roman-Catholic he wanted to show her the beauty of his faith, and gave her a pamphlet that "preached Romanism and persuaded to conversion." [2]) He made a priest show her "the fair sides of Rome and took her to "Catholic churches on solemn occasions." [3]) She, however, could not possibly like his religion, and the hero, understanding he could not win her over to his faith, said to her : "Whatever say priests or controversalists, God is good and loves all the sincere. Believe then what you can." [4]) He left Europe to spend some years in India, but before his departure he established a school for the heroine with his own money.

It was the novelist's purpose to finish the hero's life by his death at sea, but her father did not like novels which left a melancholy impression upon the mind, so she left the hero's return an open question.

This hero is the most perfect of Charlotte Brontë's creations, seen with full observation, and drawn from experience. He is a living being, in all his littleness and greatness : the image of the choleric but noble M. Héger, of whom the authoress wrote in May 1842 that he was "a man of power as to mind, but very choleric and irritable in temperament," [5]) and that an English word that she now and then introduced into her imperfect French "nearly plucks the eyes out of his head when he sees it." [6])

In none of her heroes is her ideal so keenly reflected as in this description of the man in whom she saw the personification of all the qualities she longed to see in the hero of her own thoughts. What in Rochester is a 'certain' projection of the ideal, is in Paul Emanuel the full projection.

Charlotte's heroes are no embodiments of any doctrine or opinion on morals, politics or religion. It is a fact that she had no sympathy with Roman-Catholicism, yet her best hero is a Roman-Catholic and is even brought up by Jesuits. That she was

---

[1]) ibid., p. 470. [2]) ibid., p. 477. [3]) ibid., p. 487. [4]) ibid., p. 488.
[5]) E. C. Gaskell, *Life of Chr. Brontë*, p. 153.
[6]) ibid., p. 153.

aware of her incapacity to force her opinions on others, is proved by a letter of Nov. 6th 1849 to her friend E, in which she writes: "I am no teacher ; to look on me in that way, is to mistake me. To teach is not my vocation."

Her heroes show no trace of psychological development.

None of the four heroes speaks of the then state of affairs in Europe. They never talk politics, although Charlotte herself did not lose sight of the movements of her time. With regard to the dethronement of Louis Philippe she wrote : "I remember well wishing my lot had been cast in the troubled times of the late war, and seeing in its exciting incidents a kind of stimulating charm, which it made my pulses beat fast to think of.... I have still no doubt that the shock of moral earthquakes wakens a vivid sense of life, of both nations and individuals.... That England may be spared the spasms, cramps and frenzy-fits now contorting the Continent, and threatening Ireland, I earnestly pray. With the French and Irish I have no sympathy. With the Germans and Italians I think the case is different ; as different as the love of freedom is from the lust of license." [1] What was going on in her own country failed likewise to inspire her. Though *Shirley* deals with industrial troubles, they are the troubles of the years 1830—32, and not those of her own time. A letter to some unknown friend contains the confirmation of her want of interest : "I am amused at the interest you take in politics. Don 't expect to rouse me ; to me, all ministries and all oppositions seem to be pretty much alike. D'Israeli was factious as leader of the opposition...."

She avows her incapacity of writing on social problems in a letter to her publisher : "I cannot write books handling the topic of the day.... Nor can I take up any philanthropic scheme, though I honour philanthropy ; and voluntarily and sincerely veil my face before such a mighty subject as that handled in Mrs. Beecher Stowe's work *Uncle Tom's Cabin*. To manage these

---

[1] Letter to Miss Wooler, March 31st, 1848.

great matters rightly they must be long and practically studied, their bearings known intimately and their evils felt genuinely...." [1])

It is certain that she read the works of George Sand, because she said of her : "she has a grasp of mind, which, if I cannot fully comprehend, I can very deeply respect," [2]) but it is difficult to see any influence of this French novelist in the treatment of her heroes. Harold Williams rightly observes that "the credit of directing Ch. Brontë's aims in fiction can hardly be given to the French realists : her venture was an independent leading of her own genius ; but unintentionally she was a forerunner of change." [3])

She has done away with the male perfection of Richardson and has launched an entirely new hero, "a variation of type from the usual hero with the chiselled nose, the impeccable, or if peccable, amiable character, and the general nullity." [4]) By introducing Rochester, 'the man with the past', as the hero she created a sensation and roused new interest in the novel.

It may safely be said that in all her heroes there is a germ of the same man, a woman's ideal ; but in every new one there is a growth to be seen, a perfecting of the original conception, till in Paul Emanuel the perfection is reached. In Paul Emanuel "he is reproduced for the first time with an abandonment of reticence starting in so puritan and severely restrained a character as hers." [5]) He is the personification of "the woman's longing for a strong master" [6]) as Leslie Stephen said of Rochester, a statement which is, however, applicable to all her heroes. She pictured them unattractive in appearance and made their harshness border on brutality, which is due to "her photographic fidelity to the life she knew." [7]) With the exception of Rochester, Leslie

---

[1]) Letter from Ch. Brontë to Mr. Smith, Oct. 30th, 1852.
[2]) E. C. Gaskell, *Life of Ch. Brontë*, p. 240.
[3]) H. Williams, *Modern English Writers*, p. 275.
[4]) G. Saintsbury, *Three Mid-Century Novelists*, p. 278.
[5]) J. A. Falconer, *English Studies*, April, 1927.
[6]) Leslie Stephen, *Hours in a Library*, Vol. III, p. 23.
[7]) H. Walker, *The Literature of the Victorian Era*, p. 721.

Stephen's opinion is right, viz. that Miss Brontë's heroines fall in love with men who are "embodiments of great masculine qualities — energy, honour and real generosity — under rather crusty outsides." [1])

Her experience is limited; "she could only build on what she herself had seen and heard and known, she could not create out of 'airy nothing'" [2]) and she tried to make up for what she lacked by imagination. She wanted to give pictures of real life, of men as she saw them; but unknowingly she wove into reality her own secret romantic longings. She was fully aware of her shortcomings, for when Mr. James Taylor and Mr. W. S. Williams both complained of the lack of distinctness and impressiveness in her heroes she wrote to the former: "In delineating male character I labour under disadvantages: intuition and theory will not always adequately supply the place of observation and experience. When I write about women, I am sure of my ground — in the other case I am not so sure." [3])

Though Thackeray set an example of making insignificant figures attractive by the light he throws upon their dealings, it is not possible to see any influence of this author on the treatment of Charlotte Brontë's heroes. She admired him greatly, was thankful for his hints and the criticism he thought well to bestow on her works and dedicated to him the second edition of Jane Eyre. No more is any likeness to Dickens's heroes to be traced. Prof. Saintsbury observes that "she belonged to no school" and that "she was not involved in any literary parties." [4]) She is the link between the older and the newer novelists. Her heroes reveal a return to Romanticism, but "a romanticism of individual passion, similar to that of the previous generation. The novelty lies in the quality of the soul, which shares its deeper secrets with the reader." [5])

---
[1]) L. Stephen, *George Eliot*, p. 103.
[2]) H. Walker, *The Literature of the Victorian Era*, p. 714—715.
[3]) Letter to J. Taylor, March 1st, 1849.
[4]) G. Saintsbury, *Three Mid-Century Novelists*, p. 277.
[5]) Legouis and Cazamian, *A History of English Literature*, Vol. II, Ch. VI, p. 359.

CHAPTER XI.

EMILY BRONTË (1814—1848).

Emily's life was similar to that of her sister, whom she accompanied to Brussels ; but she returned after a year already to attend to her father's household. She died at Haworth a year after her first and only novel was published. The hero of this, like those of her sister, occupies a place by himself among heroes. Charlotte's opinion of her sisters is, that : "neither Emily nor Anne was learned ; ....they wrote from the impulse of nature, the dictates of intuition and from such stores of observation as their limited experience had enabled them to amass." [1]) In her preface to *Wuthering Heights* Charlotte Brontë says that Emily never came in direct contact with the inhabitants of the district. "What her mind had gathered of the real concerning them was too exclusively confined to those tragic and terrible traits of which, in listening of the secret annals of every rude vicinage, the memory is sometimes compelled to receive the impress. Her sombre spirit at the bottom of which was 'a secret power and fire that might have informed the brain and kindled the veins of a hero' found in these stories material to create a being like Heathcliff."

This hero, the sum total of the wickedness, cruelty and harshness of all the inhabitants of the Yorkshire moors together, is a very remarkable person, as singular a being as has ever been created or described by a woman. His character is kept up throughout the book with great accuracy ; not one moment does

---

[1]) Biographical Notice to *Wuthering Heights* by Currer Bell, World's Classics ed.

Heathcliff swerve from his intentions to ruin the members of the family and their offspring, who have looked upon him with disdain and treated him as an intruder. Heathcliff, who was "rough as a saw-edge and hard as whinstone" [1]) was "a dirty, ragged blackhaired child, big enough to walk and talk," [2]) when he was found in a Liverpool street by Mr. Earnshaw and taken up into his household. He remained a favourite with his fosterfather, but was disliked by the latter's children. As soon as the son Hindley was the head of the family at his father's death, he "drove Heathcliff from his company to the servants, deprived him of the instructions of the curate and compelled him to labour out of doors as hard as any lad on the farm." [3]) Heathcliff promised himself to pay Hindley back; "I don't care how long I wait, if I can only do it at last" [4]) he said. Deprived of intellectual education, he also deteriorated in personal appearance; "he took a grim pleasure apparently, in exciting the aversion rather than the esteem of his few acquaintances." [5]) However, when the girl he was secretly in love with was married to Edgar Linton, he visited them and "his countenance.... retained no mark of former degradation" but "a half-civilised ferocity lurked yet in the depressed brows and eyes full of black fire." [6]) He hated Linton, because Catharine was married to him. Catharine, contrary to expectation, loved Heathcliff, because, as she said: "he's more myself than I am. Whatever our souls are made of, his and mine are the same." [7]) She warned her sister-in-law, who was in love with him, against him, and described him as "an unreclaimed creature, without refinement, without cultivation; an arid wilderness of furze and whinstone," who did not conceal "depths of benevolence and affection beneath a stern exterior." [8]) This "fierce, pitiless wolfish man," [9]) "a bird of bad omen," [10]) ran away with and married Linton's sister in

---

[1]) E. Brontë, *Wuthering Heights*, p. 33.
[2]) ibid., p. 35. [3]) ibid., p. 44/45. [4]) ibid., p. 60. [5]) ibid., p. 67.
[6]) ibid., p. 96. [7]) ibid., p. 80. [8]) ibid., p. 103. [9]) ibid., p. 104.
[10]) ibid., p. 105.

spite of Catharine's warnings. He led her such a hard life that she ran away from him. He then took up his abode with Hindley Earnshaw, whom he turned into a drunkard, who mortgaged his house (Heathcliffe holding the mortgage), that Hindley's son Hareton should be penniless after his death. He succeeded in ruining the whole family; he then expressed a wish about his burial, namely that he might lie during his eternal rest side by side with the woman whose image had visited and surrounded him all these years. Notwithstanding his great love for this woman, it is remarkable that there was not a spark of feeling for her only daughter, whom he also included in his hatred, most likely because she was also Linton's daughter. The only one to whom he showed some kindness was Hareton, whose "startling likeness to Catharine connected him fearfully with her," [1] whose "aspect was the ghost of (his) immortal love" [2] and who was the only one who after Heathcliff's death "sat by the corpse all night, weeping in bitter earnest." [3] For Catharine he felt an immortal love, but the scene in the death-chamber forces on the reader the question : Is this love, to rebuke a dying woman for having ruined his life because she married another ? Is this love that only so reluctantly forgives ?

Heathcliff's attraction to Catharine is not physical. Emile Montégut states so well why the heroine still loves him in spite of her union to another when he says : "ils forment à eux deux un monstre hybride, à deux sexes et à deux âmes ; il est l'âme mâle du monstre, elle en est l'âme femelle. En lui, Catharine reconnaît ses énergies non comprimées par la réserve imposée à son sexe ; en lui, elle contemple écloses comme de poétiques fleurs empoisonnées toutes ses perversités secrètes." [4] Heathcliff is painted from the outside ; the motives that led him to his inhuman deeds are not explained and can only find their cause in the harsh experiences of his youth.

On him Emily Brontë's perversity projects itself. In her youth

---

[1] ibid., p. 329. [2] ibid., p. 329. [3] ibid., p. 341.
[4] E. Montégut, *Ecrivains Modernes de l'Angleterre*, p. 352.

the authoress was most probably told some creepy tale with strongly overdone characters. She retained the figure of the hero in her imagination and revelled in inflicting pain on him or in letting him be cruel to others. When she grew older this imaginary hero kept satisfying her perverse tendencies, whilst she, increasing in age, added characteristics of a grown-up man and made him commit cruelties corresponding with his age. Mr. M. Polak's striking remark : "the origin of Heathcliff lies in the psyche of his creator ; he stands for the perverse part of the author's soul" [1]) is quite to the point. It is, however, not necessary that the authoress was a cruel woman herself. It is quite possible that she gave in to these cruelties in her thoughts and used them as material for her novel. The few vague pronouncements which might lead to the supposition of the novelist's being a perverse character are not convincing.

The present writer suggests to find the germ of this hero's character in the Bluebeard of some children's tale. In romantic fiction this savage, brutish creature is unique.

---

[1]) M. Polak, Wuthering Heights, *Neophilologus,* 14de jaargang, 1929, p. 126.

CHAPTER XII.

ELIZABETH CLEGHORN GASKELL (1810—1865).

The period in which three great feminine novelists lived, but to which we have not found a single allusion in the works of the Brontës, was one in which the public mind was agitated by the commercial and industrial troubles then dividing the nation into two classes: the Rich and the Poor. The 'rich', the manufacturers, had no other purpose than to satisfy their egoism and materialism, paying attention only to their own interests, whilst they required from their labourers the greatest amount of work at the lowest wages. The misery among the working classes, already increased by a few successive bad harvests and consequently dear bread, had now reached such a climax that riots broke out, and strikes were the order of the day. The conditions of the poor contrasted sharply with the wealth of the employers, amassed thanks to the enormous profits made by introduction of machinery and low wages.

The Reform Bill of 1832 had left the workman deprived of franchise. To get amelioration of social abuses the labourers were forced to unite and form Trade Unions. They laid their wishes down in the 'People's Charter', which led to the great Chartist-meeting of 1838 at Manchester and the next year to the rejection of the Chartist petition. The heroic march of socialism and the joint efforts of the factory-hands were rewarded by the abolition of the corn-laws, the introduction of free-trade and, in the end, admission of Labour into Parliament.

According to close witnesses of the existing conditions, the reign of egoism, without any sympathy for human suffering, could be ended only by a better understanding between employer and workman, an appreciation of the one for the other, and not be fostering revolutionary ideas. An absolute change in human relations had to be brought about. It was, as Louis Cazamian expressed it : "La naissance d'un interventionisme sentimental et conservateur, où l'émotion humaine et religieuse, alliée à l'intérêt, suggère la nation d'une solidarité sociale." [1])

Charles Dickens was the first of those novelists who tried to rouse sympathy for social reform, and declared himself an advocate for the Trades-Union. He describes in *Hard Times* the hardships of the hero, Stephen Blackpool, a factoryhand of Coketown, who for private reasons refused to join the Union of Workers called into existence as the only remedy to crush the oppressors, who lived on the results of their labour. This novel does not acquaint the reader with the state of affairs in the manufacturing towns, for the author stood too far aloof from the workman to be able to represent him and his life as it really was.

Mrs. Gaskell is the first woman-writer who has given vent to her feelings on this subject in her first two novels and who expressed : "la réaction spontanée du sentiment religieux contre un system industriel qui viole les enseignements de la Bible." [2]) She had this advantage over Dickens that she constantly met masters as well as hands, so that she was able to draw striking characters and situations.

Elizabeth Cleghorn was born on Sept. 29th 1810 at Chelsea, but spent her life at Knutsford near Manchester. At the age of twenty-two she married a Unitarian minister at Manchester and lived the rest of her life in this manufacturing town where she died from heart-failure in Nov. 1865. Being a close witness of all the struggles between 1832 and 1844, she became "a stanch defender of the rights of the distressed Lancashire operatives" [3])

---

[1]) L. Cazamian, *Le Roman Social en Angleterre*, Introduction, p. 4.
[2]) L. Cazamian, *Le Roman Social en Angleterre*, Ch. VII, p. 380.
[3]) Introduction to *North and South*, by Mrs. E. C. Gaskell.

and an eloquent cahmpion for the bringing about of a better understanding between employer and workman.

She did not make any attempt at novelwriting, until after her only son's death. In order to get over the blow her husband suggested she should try to write a novel, and the outcome of her endeavour was *Mary Barton*, published in 1847, dealing with the condition of the labouring class. She wrote from personal observation for she visited the working-people in the capacity of their minister's wife and beheld the poverty and misery with her own eyes. She had become well-acquainted with the mental and social condition of the English workingman. She knew that he was industrious, helpful, economical, and that he endured hardships and privations long before he gave vent to his discontent. In her preface to *Mary Barton*, Mrs. Gaskell says: "I had always felt a deep sympathy with the care-worn men, who looked as if doomed to struggle through their lives in strange alternations between work and want; .... A little manifestation of this sympathy... had laid open to me the hearts of one or two of the more thoughtful among them; I saw that they were sore and irritable against the rich, the even tenor of whose seeming happy lives appeared to increase the anguish caused by the lottery-like nature of their own. Whether the bitter complaints made by them, of the neglect which they experienced from the prosperous — especially from the masters whose fortunes they had helped to build up — were well-founded or no, it is not for me to judge. It is enough to say, that this belief of injustice and unkindness which they endure from their fellow-creatures, taints what might be resignation to God's will, and turns it to revenge in too many of the poor uneducated factoryworkers of Manchester." At the same time Mrs. Gaskell witnessed the manufacturers in their luxurious mansions, living a life of ease and comfort, enabled to do so by the exertions of the workmen.

Profound human sympathy and keen insight into other people's deeds and motives led her to create a hero, whose life was to be a plea for the labourer. This hero, John Barton, was "a thorough specimen of a Manchester man; born of factory workers, and himself bred up in youth, and living in manhood, among the mills. He was below the middle size and slightly made; there was almost a stunted look about him; and his wan, colourless face gave you the idea that in his childhood he had suffered from the scanty living consequent upon bad times and improvident habits. His features were strongly marked, though not irregular, and their expression was extreme earnestness; resolute either for good or evil." [1]) With the death of his wife in childbed "one of the good influences over John Barton's life had departed." [2]) All the misery and sorrow he had experienced from a boy, had made him morose and obstinate. He was strongly attached to his daughter whom "he humoured with tender love." [3]) Many a time he had helped a friend in need, even at his own expense. Like so many others in similar cases, his grief led him "to public activity, made him readier to adopt the miseries of others as his own and enlarged his resentment against their common causes." [4]) He turned Chartist and was one of "the lifeworn, gaunt, anxious, hunger-stamped men," [5]) who were delegated to London, glad that "he was one of those chosen to be instruments in making known the distress of the people." [6]) He refused to accept the often told story that the rich did not know the condition of the poor. "If they don't know, they ought to know" [7]) he said. He returned even more embittered by what he had seen and experienced. His mind became occupied with one overpowering thought: "Why are men so separate, when God has made them all? It is not His Will that their interests are so far apart." [8])

On the occasion of a strike a petition was handed to the employers'-committee, of which his own employer's son was the chairman. This man insulted the workmen, among whom was

---

[1]) E. C. Gaskell, *Mary Barton,* Everyman's Library, p. 5.
[2]) ibid., p. 20.   [3]) ibid., p. 20.
[4]) W. Minto in the *Fortnightly Review,* Juli—Dec., 1878.
[5]) E. C. Gaskell, *Mary Barton,* p. 80.
[6]) ibid., p. 80.   [7]) ibid., p. 9.   [8]) ibid., p. 432.

Barton, so much that they decided to murder him. They cast lots and it fell to Barton's share to filful the dreadful mission. After the deed was done mental misery was added to the physical. When old Carson, the father of the murdered man, discovered that Barton was the murderer and wanted to hand him to the police to be hanged, he laid all his pent-up misery in the words : "Death, Lord, what is it to life ? To such a life as I've been leading this fortnight past ?"[1] "God above only can tell the agony with which I've repented me of it.... As for hanging, that's just nought at all."[2] Carson sobbed out his grief and then Barton saw in him a fellow-sufferer ; he who himself had known the loss of his only son, had caused the same sorrow to another. He saw "no longer the enemy, the oppressor" in his employer, but "a very poor, and desolate old man,"[3] a father like himself, borne down with misery. "Now he knew that no good thing could come of this evil."[4] In Carson's heart rose pity for "the poor wasted skeleton of a man, the smitten creature who had told him of his sin, and implored his pardon."[5] He went to Barton's house the next day to forgive the murderer of his son, just in time, for a few minutes later the workman "lay a corpse in Mr. Carson's arms."[6]

It was not Mrs. Gaskell's purpose to offer John Barton as 'a fair representative of the artisans and factory operatives of Manchester' as Mr. Greg, the critic of the *Edinburgh Review* supposed. The present writer is glad to agree with Prof. Minto, who rightly observes that Mrs. Gaskell did not want "to convey the impression that the mass of the factory-workers were like John Barton in his passionate hatred of the rich masters" but that he was "one figure in a broad picture of varied life."[7] If Carson had not considered his workmen as 'tool-using animals', but had had a fatherly regard for them and had explained to them the reasons why he was forced to cut down their wages,

---

[1] ibid., p. 343.   [2] ibid., p. 344.   [3] and.   [4] ibid., p. 346.
[5] ibid., p. 349.   [6] ibid., p. 351.
[7] *Fortnighthly Review*, July—Dec., 1878.

they would have understood to what they owed their misery and would have endured it with more resignation. It is Mr. Montégut who states that in most books of his time it says "que l'homme n'est pas seulement une machine à production matérielle, qu'il n'est pas fait pour l'absolutisme et l'anarchie qu'il n'a pas été déstiné.... à l'esclavage et.... à la révolte, mais qu'il a été prédestiné à un but plus noble et plus complet, à être soumis et indépendant tout ensemble, raisonnable et religieux tout ensemble, dévoué à ses semblables et inflexible dans la juste revendication et la libre possession de ses droits." [1]
"It is not to die, or even to die of hunger, that makes a man wretched.... But it is to live miserable we know not why ; to work sore and yet gain nothing ; to be heart-worn, weary.... ; it is to die slowly all our life long imprisoned in a deaf, dead Infinite Injustice...." [2] with these words Thomas Carlyle gave his opinion on the condition of the labourer. In his article in the *Forthnightly Review* Dec. 1878, Prof. Minto supposes that Mrs. Gaskell was prompted to write *Mary Barton* after she had read Disraeli's 'Sybil'. However, he adds : "When I say that *Mary Barton* was probably suggested by *Sybil*, I do not of course intend to detract from Mrs. Gaskell's originality, to represent her as an imitator or plagiarist, or even to imply that she was moved to write by a conscious spirit of emulation.... She may not have read *Sybil* at all." If Mrs. Gaskell borrowed at all, she gave anyhow the solution of the problem in a more sympathic way than Dickens or Disraeli. The only traceable aim that they all three have in common is propagandism for an improvement of existing social evils.

The employers were also of opinion that they were misunderstood. "Because we don't explain our reasons, they won't believe we're acting reasonably" [3] they said. So Mrs. Gaskell thought it her duty to make the position of the employers also

---
[1] E. Montégut, *Ecrivains Modernes de l'Angleterre*, Deuxième Série, p. 8.
[2] Th. Carlyle, *Past and Present*, Collins' Classics, p. 233.
[3] E. C. Gaskell, *North and South*, Everyman's Library, p. 111.

better understood, a subject which she took in hand in her second novel, published in 1855. For the hero of *North and South* she took the average manufacturer, and succeeded in portraying this self-made man so naturally that Sir W. Fairbairn, an engineer at Manchester, wrote to her : "I have to thank you for having thus raised the standard of the manufacturing character above that of sordid grain ; and I look forward to the time, when higher motives than the mere acquisition of money will actuate the powers as well as the industry of our more intelligent and active manufacturers. Your work has that tendency and will elevate the character and effect a closer union between intellect and industry than has hitherto subsisted amongst us." [1)

Thornton, the hero, was "a tall, broad-shouldered man of about thirty — with a face that was neither plain nor handsome," [2) but on which there was "an expression of resolution and power." [3) He was a man of the heroic type, generous, open-minded, just, the very representative of the self-made man, the "architect of his own fortunes." [4) By incessant work and self-denial he had been able to pay off all his late father's debts. [5) The other manufacturers of his town looked up to him "for his prompt and ready wisdom" [6) and regarded him "as a man of great force and character ; of power in many ways." [7) The purpose of his life was to gain money, because of the authority it gives, and "to hold and maintain a high, honourable place among the merchants of his country — the men of his town." [8) He lived in a simple style in the continual work and din of his factory. He loved his work for work's sake, for it was exertion and not enjoyment that gave a zest to life. Thornton would rather be a man "toiling, suffering, — nay, failing and successless, than lead a dull prosperous life." [9) He was very proud of belonging to a town that had produced the man that invented the steam-hammer,

---

[1) Letter from Sir W. Fairbairn to Mrs. Gaskell, June 6, 1855.
[2) E. C. Gaskell, *North and South*, p. 59.
[3) ibid., p. 59.   [4) ibid., p. 407.   [5) ibid., p. 82.   [6) ibid., p. 204.
[7) ibid., p. 156.   [8) ibid., p. 108.   [9) ibid., p. 76.

"the practical realisation of a gigantic thought." [1]) He hated state-interference and had his mill altered before the bill was passed which forced the manufacturers to alter the chimneys so as to consume their own smoke; "else," he said, "I should have given all the trouble in yielding that I legally could." [2]) In his mill he wanted to be the autocratic ruler during working-time. He considered it a degradation to his workmen, if he interfered with them after working-hours. "Because they labour ten hours a day for us, I do not see that we have any right to impose leading-strings upon them for the rest of their time" [3]) he said. Consequently, he was not acquainted with their way of living and what they could do with their wages. His opinion was that a workman has his own future in his hands, that "a working-man may raise himself into the power and position of a master by his own exertions and behaviour; that, in fact, every one who rules himself to decency and sobriety of conduct, and attention to his duties, comes to our (the masters') ranks." [4]) His workmen did not love him. They called him "a bull-dog on hind-legs, dressed up in coat and breeches." [5]) Although he was not unkind or inflexible by nature, his own working hard constantly and his power of seeing only the progress of trade blinded him to the misery of the workers. The preceding quotations show to the full the employer's character with all his ambition and energy, a fair example of that race of enterprising self-made men that made England's industry and trade great after the Napoleonic wars.

The good qualities of his character were stirred up by the influence of Margaret Hale, [6]) who brought him into direct contact with one of his workmen. The first step he took, when he had become acquainted with the poverty of the factory-hands, was the establishment of a cooperative kitchen where he took his meal with his workman on the opening-day to please them and by this won their good favour. He was in love with Margaret,

---

[1]) ibid., p. 75. [2]) ibid., p. 77. [3]) ibid., p. 116. [4]) ibid., p. 78.
[5]) ibid., p. 129. [6]) ibid., p. 117.

who rejected him because of his harsh ideas. Hidden under material interests was "a deeper religion binding him to God" [1]) which enabled him to understand Mr. Hale's sorrow after his wife's death even better dan did Margaret. She gradually learned to know him as a thoroughly reliable and sensitive nature, and to like him for his force and his tenderness. Through a strike he suffered great financial losses. He borrowed money to pay his operatives because he did not want to dismiss them, and did not despair, but "exerted himself day and night to foresee and to provide for all emergencies." [2]) At last, however, he had to stop his mill, though by a risky speculation he might have succeeded in keeping it going. He did not want to risk his creditor's money at the expense of his peace of conscience, and decided to give up his position as a master and to become a manager somewhere. [3]) Through his marriage to Margaret, who had inherited a large capital and had learned to love him very much for his noble character, he was prevented from executing his plan.

By the conception of this hero's character and his life the reader gets to know how, living in apparent luxury, the employer also has to fight his struggle for existence, though on a larger scale than the workman, who is blinded by the outward show of wealth. But "a genuine understanding by the upper classes of society what it is that the under classes intrinsically mean ; a clear interpretation of the thought which at heart torments these wild inarticulate souls, struggling there, with inarticulate uproar, like dumb creatures in pain, unable to speak what is in them" [4]) was wanted to make the employer see the necessity of better wages.

The authoress betrays fine psychological insight in the description of the lives of these two different human beings : John Barton, a simple, but noble, generous and industrious factoryhand, who through constant adversity and disappointment has

---

[1]) ibid., p. 267.   [2]) ibid., p. 409.   [3]) ibid., p. 412.
[4]) Th. Carlyle, *Chartism*, ed. New York 1856, p. 309.

gradually grown so embittered, that he perpetrates a murder without even reflecting on the consequences of his deed ; and Thornton, who is "not faultless, but fair-minded and under all the hardness of his exterior, human to the core." [1])

By taking her heroes from her immediate surroundings, Mrs. Gaskell tried to explain to either party what in her opinion was the cause of the existing discontent, viz. unacquaintance with each other's difficulties and struggles rather than man's degeneration. By giving an insight into the lives of both employer and workman she wanted to rouse mutual sympathy. It had to lead the employer to a fair reward of the workman's daily toil ; it had to convince the labourer that the manufacturer also has a life of work and difficulties, and that for everyone "Work is the mission of man in this earth," [2]) which is "un fait éminemment social, capable de réunir les hommes par des lieux moraux et hiérarchiques, un fait qui, à la longue, ronge tout égoïsme, brise les intérêts individuels, si fort qu'ils soient, et les réduit à n'être plus qu'un anneau de la grande chaîne qui enveloppe la société et fait dépendre l'homme de l'homme." [3])

"All Mrs. Gaskell's novels except *Sylvia's Lovers* were based on her actual experience of life" writes Esther Alice Chadwick in the introduction to this book. She continues : "In *Sylvia's Lovers*, published in 1863, the authoress took an entirely new departure in writing a historical novel." Though it is a historical novel, the hero's life, described unto moral edification, is entirely what the life of any young shopkeeper in any town of England might have been. Through the description of this life the authoress wants to show to what a pitiful end one may come if one does not heed the commandmend : "Thou shalt not bear false witness against thy neighbour," even if it be from some noble motive, and certainly not if it proceeds from mere egoism, as is the case with Philip Raeburn.

---

[1]) H. Walker, *The Literature of the Victorian Era*, p. 725.
[2]) Th. Carlyle, *Chartism*, p. 319.
[3]) E. Montégut, *Ecrivains Modernes de l'Angleterre*, Deuxième Série, p. 128.

The description of the hero does not make a very agreeable impression on the reader. He was "a serious-looking young man, tall, but with a slight stoop in his shoulders, brought on by his occupation; he had thick hair standing off from his forehead in a peculiar but not unpleasing manner; a long face, with a slight aquiline nose, dark eyes, and a long upper lip, which gave a disagreeable aspect to his face." [1] He was greatly in love with his cousin Sylvia, but his "rare and constant love deserved a better fate than it met with." [2] She did not like him because of his pre-possession and his pedantic way of expressing himself. On his way to London on business, he saw his more successful rival in love, Charles Kinraid, empressed by a press-gang and carried away. Kinraid saw Philip and asked him to tell Sylvia that he was sure to come back and that he considered her his betrothed. Philip answered "something inarticulately" [3] and afterwards made himself believe that he had not promised anything. After his return from London he did not say a word about Kinraid's message. Sylvia's father got into difficulties and was put to death in spite of Philip's endeavours and sacrifices of money to save the old man from the gallows. Sylvia was benumbed by the shock and having heard that Kinraid was drowned, accepted Philip's proposal of marriage. She refused to doff her black dress for the wedding-day, so that Philip had "to wed his long-sought bride in morning-raiment." [4] Though he gradually learned to see that she did not love him, he remained good to her and "with the patient perseverance that was one remarkable feature in his character, he went on striving to deepen and increase her love when most other men would have given up the endeavour. [5] On the day he consented to call his first-born daughter after his mother-in-law, he perhaps "reached the zenith of life's happiness," [6] for then "she lifted up her pale face from the pillow and put up her lips to be kissed." [7] In his

---

[1] E. C. Gaskell, *Sylvia's Lovers*, Everyman's Library, p. 21—22.
[2] ibid., p. 111.   [3] ibid., p. 190.   [4] ibid., p. 292.   [5] ibid., p. 294.
[6] ibid.; p. 303.   [7] ibid., p. 303.

business he prospered, having "the perseverance, the capability for head-work and calculation, the steadiness and general forethought which might have made him a great merchant if he had lived in a large city...." [1]) One day Kinraid returned and the secret was revealed, which Philip had dreaded all these years. To his wife he explained why he had not delivered the message : "He did not love you as I did.... I might ha' given you his message, but I heard those speaking of him, who knew him so well ; they talked of his false fickle ways. How was I to know he would keep true to thee... I have loved you as no man but me ever loved you." [2]) Her scorn and hatred were too much for him. He left her and enlisted as a volunteer in the navy. One day he saved in a battle a man, who appeared to be Kinraid. Being afterwards wounded himself, he was sent to England where he lived in his native town unrecognised. He chanced to save his own child from being drowned and through this accident he met his wife again, whose forgiveness he implores. "Child," said he, "I ha' made thee my idol ; and if I could live my life o'er again I would love my God more, and thee less ; and then I shouldn't have sinned this sin against thee." [3]) He died with his wife's kiss on his lips and her arms around him.

Philip's life is intended as an illustration of Mrs. Gaskell's saying : 'All deeds however hidden and long passed by have their eternal consequences', thus showing herself a disciple of Carlyle, who says : "the first of all Gospels in this, that a Lie cannot endure for ever." [4]) Later on Comte in his *Philosophy of Necessity* published in 1841 puts it thus : 'misery will follow injustice with the same certainty that a stone set free from the hand will fall to earth...." Philip's failure to convey the message caused him a life of unrest, disappointment and an untimely death; his good deeds, his great love for Sylvia procured for him, though on his deathbed, the certainty that his wife had learned to value and love him. To live a life, even though it be one of

---

[1]) ibid., p. 310.   [2]) ibid., p. 327.   [3]) ibid., p. 424.
[4]) Th. Carlyle, *The French Revolution*, Vol. I, p. 41.

cares and troubles, with a conscience at peace is the greatest blessing and without it no perfect happiness is possible. However, Mrs. Gaskell's description of the eternal consequence of a lie is too strongly coloured, especially the end e. g. Philip's return and reconciliation to his wife.

This novelist showed the consequences of one evil deed in a life full of unrest. Later on George Eliot will picture an existence wrecked owing to transgression.

Resuming, we may conclude that Mrs. Gaskell's heroes, no more than Charlotte Brontë's, betray a return to the hero of the first female experimenters. The old sentimentality had its day ; the former hero's picture of perfection had been replaced by a representation of an ordinary human being. The spirit of the age required a character of a nature different from the woman's ideal of more than half a century before and Mrs. Gaskell also gratified the general demand. Though all her heroes are men of noble, generous characters, they do not manifest these good qualities in the exaggerated manner of Richardson's hero. Their nobility and generosity is often concealed behind a screen of harshness, of sorrow, of embitterment. Mrs. Gaskell understood the emotions of her fellow-people and looked through their outward disguises. She read their hidden thoughts and was able to explain their actions and motives. She let her heroes move in their own worlds among people of their own rank and standing, and made them speak in their own dialect and in their own way. This is confirmed by Louis Cazamian who states : "Les héros de Mrs. Gaskell ont plus d'une réalité générale et typique ; leur physionomie est locale ; leurs paroles offrent ce mélange de naïveté et d'humour qui passe pour le trait distinctif du Lancashire." [1] The characters, manners and language of her heroes are based on "concrete observation, and quite close to the view of reality which one can expect from a woman's frank, tender, and yet penetrating glance." [2]

---

[1] L. Cazamian, Le Roman Social en Angleterre, Ch. VII, p. 401.
[2] Legouis and Cazamian, A History of English Literature, Vol. II, Bk. VI, Ch. III, p. 357.

Mrs. Gaskell had far greater opportunities of meeting people in their daily occupations than had Charlotte Brontë. The latter also based her heroes' characters on reality, but it was a reality mixed with romanticism, or helped by fantasy and greatly under the influence of her heart's ideal. So Mrs. Gaskell was in advance of Charlotte Brontë. She is the first novelist who introduced psychological realism into the description of her hero's character though her psychology did not go very deep. Her delineation of character was still immature. There was a growth of personality, though small, but not based on great inward struggles. This novelist possessed what is the basis of psychology and what enabled her to read her characters : 'Cette sympathie de l'intelligence éclairée par l'amour, qui descend doucement et se met sans faste à la portée de ceux qu'elle veut comprendre."[1] The lives of Mrs. Gaskell's heroes still rouse sympathy and are, even for present-day readers, interesting characters.

---

[1] F. Brunetière, *Le Roman Naturaliste,* p. 286.

CHAPTER XIII.

GEORGE ELIOT (1819—1880).

The introduction of psychology into the delineation of her heroes' characters, which was begun by Mrs. Gaskell, was continued by George Eliot with increasing success.

George Eliot's life was very different from the lives of preceding women-novelists. Her intuition was assisted by a constant study of psychology, and so it is a matter of course that her insight into character, her understanding of the human heart goes deeper than that of Mrs. Gaskell, who was enabled to do so by her intuition only. She expresses in her novels, what her contemporary Robert Browning wove into his poetry: a representation of the struggles of a soul and a revelation of the motives, impulses and hereditary influences which cause human actions.

Mary Ann Evans, as was George Eliot's maiden name, was born on November 22 1819 at Arbury Farm in Warwickshire. After some months the family removed to Griff where her father was the agent of a large estate. Here she spent the first twenty years of her life, studying classical and modern languages assiduously. With no person in the neighbourhood could she discuss the intellectual and spiritual problems that began to absorb her interest. She was essentially religious, but lived in a time when religion had ceased to be the stay and solace of mankind and she did not find satisfaction in existing creeds. Leslie Stephen in his work on George Eliot says: "when asked who unsettled her orthodoxy, George Eliot answered 'Scott. The qualities he admires — manliness, patriotism, unflinching loyalty, and purity of life — are to be found equally among

Protestants and Catholics, Roundheads and Cavaliers. The wide sympathy which sees good and bad on all sides makes it difficult to accept any version of the doctrine which supposes salvation to be associated with the acceptance of a dogma.' " [1])

Through a quarrel with her father she went to stay some time at Coventry, at the house of Charles Bray, an agnostic, the author of *The Philosophy of Necessity*. Bray's preaching had much in common with the tenets of positivism, viz.: "that we should teach men that goodness and justice, truthfulness and purity of life, do not rest on the mysterious revelations of this or that prophet, but on laws of nature." [2]) He was the first that had great influence on her way of thinking and may claim "to have laid the base of that philosophy, which she afterwards retained." [3]) Through him she came to freedom of inquiry. Her loss of faith had deprived her of a support in life. She devoted herself to thinking and examining, for she wanted to go deeper and deeper into the mysteries of life and understand its complexity better.

She easily came under the influence of Comte, who in his *Philosophie Positive* had no other purpose than 'to present all the principal truths affecting man's life in an orderly series, and to show that laws and conditions of spiritual health were precisely of the same positive, scientific, ascertainable kind as the laws of his bodily health.' At length she became a pupil of Herbart Spencer, whose idealistic conception of purpose and duty she accepted as the highest expression of all morality.

She came to the conclusion that "Our deeds determine us as much as we determine our deeds ; and until we know who has been or will be the peculiar combination of outward with inward facts, which constitutes a man's critical actions, it will be better not to think ourselves wise about his character." [4])

After her father's death she went to live in London where, in 1848, she became a contributor to the Westminster Review,

---

[1]) Leslie Stephen, *George Eliot*, English Men of Letters, p. 27.
[2]) Charles Bray, *Phases of Opinion and Experience during a long Life*, p. 93.
[3]) ibid., p. 35.
[4]) G. Eliot, *Adam Bede*, Nelson's ed., p. 343.

a monthly on the leading philosophical and theological thoughts. Here she met John Stuart Mill and Herbart Spencer through whose intermediary she was introduced to the man who was to play such an important part in her life, George Henry Lewes, the editor of *the Leader*. His married life was unhappy. He lived separated from his wife whom he could not divorce. Miss Evans fell in love with him and defied public opinion by living with him as his wife until his death in 1878. From that time she led again a lonely life. A year after Lewes's death she married Mr. J. W. Cross who published her "Life and Letters" after her death on the 22nd of Dec. 1880.

Lewes, who was a keen, well-known critic, discovered through her journalistic writings 'her true genius' and insisted upon her setting herself to write. When she was thirty-seven years old the first offspring of her literary talents appeared under the pseudonym of George Eliot which led to the supposition that the author was a man. In the works of her first period, which are based on personal experience, her principle of human sympathy reigns supreme. In her diary J. W. Cross wrote during her illness: "It was often in her mind and on her lips that the only worthy end of all learning, of all science, of all life in fact, is, that human beings should love one another better." [1]

The purpose of her writing which she stated herself after having finished *Adam Bede* is: 'to make other people able to feel and to imagine the pains and joys of those who differ from themselves in everything but the broad fact of being struggling, erring human creatures'. She wanted to interpret character, not record the glorious deeds of heroes, which attract the attention of the public at large, but the heroic deeds which the world does not see, of a plain man, one "of a whole order of souls who, ...are spiritually complex, torn by scruples, and by the anguish of moral conflicts" [2] and the great influence he exercises

---

[1] J. W. Cross, *Life of George Eliot*, Vol. III, p. 429.
[2] Legouis and Cazamian, *A History of English Literature*, Vol. II, Bk. VI, Ch. V, p. 405.

on his surroundings. That is why she took for her heroes men, living in the world around her. "There are few prophets in the world, few sublimely beautiful women, few heroes. I can't afford to give all my love and reference to such rarities : I want a great deal of those feelings for my every-day fellow-men, especially for the few in the foreground of the great multitude whose faces I know, whose hands I touch, for whom I have to make way with kindly courtesy." [1])

Her keen observation, her intuition and her knowledge of the inner-self made her especially fitted "to give a faithful account of men and things as they have mirrored themselves in her [my] mind." [2]) The heroes of the three sketches with which she entered upon her literary career, are all clergymen by whom she wishes "to rouse sympathy for figures, who at first sight repel the more cultivated and intelligent, but who.... have all their romances, indicative of true and tender natures beneath the superficial court of old-fashioned oddities." [3])

The first is Amos Barton, the poor curate of Shepperton, who was quite unable to understand his parishioners and did not know to bring the gospel home to them. At tea-parties they talked of him as being entirely unfit for his task. [4]) The description of his person betrays an uninteresting character : "his narrow face of no particular complexion, with features of no particular shape, and an eye of no particular expression, is surmounted by a slope of baldness gently rising from brow to crown." [5]) This utterly insignificant creature, who behaved "with asinine stupidity of conduct" [6]) towards one of his distinguished parishioners, had a wife, who constantly struggled to make both ends meet, and six children. However inferior he might be as their spiritual guide, general sympathy was felt for the man at his wife's death. "There were standing men and women in that churchyard

---

[1]) G. Eliot, *Adam Bede*, p. 195.
[2]) ibid., p. 191.
[3]) Leslie Stephen, *George Eliot*, Ch. IV, p. 60.
[4]) G. Eliot, *Scenes of Clerical Life*, Collins' ed., p. 13.
[5]) ibid., p. 20.   [6]) ibid., p. 20.

who had bandied vulgar jests about their pastor, and who had lightly charged him with sin ; but now.... he was consecrated anew by his great sorrow, and they looked at him wit respectful pity." [1]) This sympathy of the parishioners bound him to them. When after a year he had to leave Shepperton because his duties as a curate were finished, there was "general regret among the parishioners : not that any of them thought his spiritual gifts pre-eminent, or was conscious of great edification from his ministry. But his recent troubles had called out their better sympathies, and that is always a source of love." [2])

"The revulsion of feeling towards Amos is capitally drawn"[3]) the publisher wrote to G. H. Lewes. George Eliot awakened through the description of this hero's loss and sorrow the reader's sympathy for the dullest and most commonplace of men.

The second hero, Mr. Gilfil, is a generally esteemed old parson "with hair around a pale and venerable face." [4]) At his death all his parishioners were present at his funeral. It was not his sermons that had brought about this, for he did not give himself the trouble of delivering a new one each Sunday, but took one from "a large heap of short sermons, rather yellow and worn at the edges." [5]) These sermons were not of "a highly doctrinal, still less of a polemical, cast. They perhaps did not search the conscience very powerfully ;.... they made no unreasonable demand on the Shepperton intellect." [6]) He was liked for his kindness, his social intercourse and his fellow-feeling. "No man knew more than the vicar about the breed of cows and horses" [7]) and when talking to his farmers he used "to approximate his accent and mode of speech to theirs." [8]) The oldest inhabitants could remember the day, when he had brought his young Italian wife home. She had died after a short time and he had never spoken of her since that day. The great love he once bore to his deceased

---

[1]) ibid., p. 88.   [2]) ibid., p. 93.
[3]) Letter from John Blackwood to G. H. Lewes, Nov. 12th, 1856.
[4]) George Eliot, *Scenes of Clerical Life*, p. 109.
[5]) ibid., p. 106.   [6]) ibid., p. 106.   [7]) ibid., p. 104.   [8]) ibid., p. 105.

bride he henceforth bestowed on his parishioners, sharing their joys and sorrows. George Eliot comments on this as follows: "In the gray-haired man who filled his pocket with sugar-plums for the little children, whose most biting words were directed against the evil-doing of the rich man,.... there was.... the same brave, faithful, tender nature that had poured out the finest, freshest forces of its life-current in a first and only love." [1]

The hero of the third story is Mr. Tryan, a zealous Evangelical clergyman who suffered from consumption and was opposed by the adherents of Mr. Crewe, the vicar of the village. However, "he fronted his opponents manfully" [2] and was fully convinced of the victory of a noble purpose. Janet Dempster, the wife of his most hateful opponent, was attracted to him when she overheard a conversation between him and a consumptive girl whom he tried to comfort with words that spoke his own sorrows. She turned to him when she could not bear any longer the hard life her husband led her. He, who could speak from his own experience, succeeded in restoring her trust in the Divine Guide. "The blessed influence of one human soul upon another" [3] is beautifully pictured here. Tryan's influence proves to be so great that Janet, whose husband died, and who now loved Tryan, was even able to continue her life, when death took her beloved clergyman from her. The man who could do this "must have been one whose heart beat with true compassion, and whose lips were moved by fervent faith." [4] "It is not perfection that makes Tryan a true hero any more than it made Luther or Bunyan, nor is it what he achieved, but in the spirit in which he sought to achieve, that lies the value of his endeavour." [5] Tryan is not a portrait of any clergyman, as George Eliot said herself, but "there are few clergyman who would be depreciated by an identification with Mr. Tryan." [6]

---

[1] ibid., p. 250.   [2] ibid., p. 329.
[3] *Cambridge History* XIII, p. 388.
[4] G. Eliot, *Scenes of Clerical Life*, p. 456.
[5] ibid., note 3.
[6] Letter from G. Eliot to John Blackwood, 17 Aug.1857.

George Eliot's purpose in drawing the lives of these three clergyman was to show that, however insignificant a man may be, though his life be one of struggles and sorrow, it is sympathy that links him to his fellow-men, it may be by giving or by receiving it. For "it is neither the cloth nor the respectability of the man himself that entitles him to goodwill, but the human anguish of his experiences — the pathos of an ordinary soul... [1] The novelist's own commentary on the lives of these heroes is very appropriate : "I wish to stir your sympathy with commonplace troubles — to win your tears for real sorrow : sorrow such as may live next door to you — such as walks neither in rags nor in velvet, but in very ordinary decent apparel." [2]

The description of these heroes reveals a much deeper insight into human character than Mrs. Gaskell's. The hero of George Eliot's first real novel is another and still better proof of it.

This hero is quite a different kind of man. If it had been the author's intention to stand up for the workman she could not have given a better example than Adam Bede. This craftsman is a character, that only now and then turns up in the modern novel. He was not an average man," but one of those, who "make their way upward, rarely as geniuses, most commonly as painstaking, honest men, with the skill and conscience to do well the tasks that lie before them," [3] "un de ces hommes, qui font humblement et modestement la grosse besogne de ce monde, un de ces hommes sans lesquels la terre serait moins verte qu'elle ne l'est." [4] In the personal description of Adam the reader gets the impression of an energetic powerful man whose mental disposition was in harmony with his physical. "A large boned, muscular man, nearly six feet high, broadchested," who in "his tall stalwartness was a Saxon, ...but the jet-black hair... and the keen glance of the dark eyes that shone under strongly-marked, prominent, and mobile eyebrows, indicated a mixture

---
[1] *Cambridge History* XIII, p. 388.
[2] George Eliot, *Scenes of Clerical Life*, Ch. VII, p. 74.
[3] G. Eliot, *Adam Bede*, p. 233.
[4] E. Montégut, *Ecrivains Modernes de l'Angleterre*, p. 46.

of Celtic blood. His face was large and roughly hewn, and when in repose had no other beauty than such as belongs to an expression of goodhumoured, honest intelligence." [1]) He was the embodiment of Carlyle's opinion that "Work is the great cure of all Misery" [2]) for, as Adam Bede said himself : "it gives you a grip hold o'things outside your own lot." [3]) He was angry with his father for not finishing a coffin that was ordered, and immediately set to work to do what his father neglected. George Eliot pictures the mixture of feelings that passed through Adam in doing so : the anger with his father's drunkenness and remembrances of the good mild father of his younger years to whom he and his brother had looked up with admiration. When the next morning his father was found drowned, he accused himself of harshness, of only having worked for his father because he liked work, of never having been able to compel himself to be kind to him, so that it was his egoism that had forced him to do what was easiest for him. He had not understood his father ; it was "his too little fellow-feeling with the weakness that errs in spite of foreseen consequences. There is but one way in which a strong determined soul can learn it — by getting his heartstrings bound round the weak and erring, so that he must share not only the outward consequences of their error, but their inward suffering." [4]) The authoress wants to show how an error committed, a kindness neglected, will haunt a conscientious person if he becomes aware of his shortcomings.

Adam Bede also fully reflects George Eliot's opinions on religion. This religion was built on a philosophical foundation. The hero did not trouble his mind about the doctrines of Dissenters and other sects, because all they profess and all their quarrels about texts is not religion. "I've seen pretty clear ever since I was a young un, as religion's something else besides doctrines and notions.... I began to see as all this weighing

---

[1]) G. Eliot, *Adam Bede,* p. 2.
[2]) Th. Carlyle, *Inaugural Speech at Edinburgh,* 2nd April 1866.
[3]) G. Eliot, *Adam Bede,* p. 124.
[4]) ibid., p. 229.

and sifting what this text means and that text means, and whether folks are saved all by God's grace, or whether there goes an ounce o' their own will to 't, was no part o' real religion at all. You may talk o' these things for hours on end, and you'll only be all the more coxy and conceited for 't. [1]) "I know a man must have the love o' God in his soul, and the Bible's God's word. But what does the Bible say? Why, it says as God put his sperrit into the workman as built the tabernacle, to make him do all the carved work and things as wanted a nice hand. And this is my way o' looking at it : there's the sperrit o' God in all things and all times — weekday as well as Sunday — and i' the great works and inventions, and i' the figuring and the mechanics. And God helps us with our headpieces and our hands as with our souls; and if a man does bits o' jobs out o' working hours — builds a oven for's wife to save her from going to the bakehouse, or scrats at his bit o' garden and makes two potatoes grow instead o' one — he's doing more good, and he's just as near to God, as if he was running after some preacher and a-praying and a-groaning." [2]) He preferred "to be humble before the mysteries o' God's dealings." [3]) As a believer in dreams and prognostics he remembered to his dying-day the mysterious, repeated raps of the willow-wand that foretold his father's death. He was of a loving and trusting nature, which "depends for so much of its happiness on what it can believe and feel about others." [4]) That is the reason why he was so sorely disappointed in the squire's son who had played with Hetty Sorel with whom Adam was in love. He hoped that the girl would turn from this man and fix her heart on him, if not, he must "put up with it whichever way it is.... I am not th' only man that 's got to do without much happiness i' this life. There's many a good bit o' work done with a sad heart. It 's God's will, and that's enough for us." [5]) At last Hetty promised to become his wife. A few days before her wedding-day the bride ran away

---

[1]) ibid., p. 199.   [2]) ibid., p. 6.   [3]) ibid., p. 199.   [4]) ibid., p. 323.
[5]) ibid., p. 355.

from home, being with child. She murdered the child. The deed was found out. To the last moment Adam stood in the Court of Justice to be near her. When she was sentenced to lifelong imprisonment the squire's son came to him to ask forgiveness for the wrong he had done him. At first Adam did not want to listen; then he fought with himself, a struggle not to be easily decided. "Facile natures, whose emotions have little permanence, can hardly understand how much resistance he overcame before he... said: 'I'm hard — it's in my nature. I was too hard with my father for doing wrong.... I've known what it is in my life to repent and feel it 's too late: I felt I'd been too harsh to my father, when he was gone from me — I feel it now, when I think of him. I've no right to be hard towards them as have done wrong and repent.... I wouldn't shake hands with you once, sir, when you asked me; but if you're willing to do it now, for all I refused then....' " [1])

This inward struggle George Eliot pictures in a most effective way. We see before us the penitent Arthur, the Squire's son, and Adam bravely struggling to surmount the antipathy to this man who had bereaved him of all his happiness. Adam's forgiveness is something great, something that rouses admiration. It is one of the novelist's ideas of religion: the complete annulment of self and participation in some common misery.

Adam bore his sorrow heroically, working hard and enjoying his work which "had always been part of his religion, and from his early days he saw clearly that good carpentry was God's will." [2]) His old neighbour's word of comfort for all his grief, that "good may come out of this that we don 't see" [3]) came true after two years. Though Adam saw only a future before him of hard working "with growing contentment and intensity of interest," [4]) there was a better future in store for him on the day that Dinah Morris promised to become his wife.

This change in Adam's mental disposition such a short time

---

[1]) ibid., p. 513. [2]) ibid., p. 532. [3]) ibid., p. 501. [4]) ibid., p. 532.

after Hetty's condemnation, draws forth Sir A. W. Ward's question : "Could a deep and noble nature such as Adam Bede's have forgotten his love for Hetty, while she was still suffering from guilt ?" [1]) It was not in Adam's nature to forget this girl so soon, for "tender and deep as his love for Hetty had been — so deep that the roots of it would never be torn away — his love for Dinah.... was the outgrowth of that fuller life which had come to him from acquaintance with deep sorrow." [2])

Adam Bede is the hero in whom we see Carlyle's influence on the authoress. He represents by his way of living the same resignation to the inevitable, the same putting full trust in God, and the same devotion of energy to work, instead of indulgence in his sorrows as Diogenes Teufelsdröckh in *Sartor Resartus*. By applying Carlyle's motto "Work and Despair not" or "Do the duty that liest nearest to yow" [3]) he finds happiness through sorrow and affliction. "Il a la carrure physique et morale des forts, l'allure assurée des caractères qui savent s'imposer et dont la vertu porte des fruits." [4]) Spencer in his *Data of Ethics* points out the obligation of behaving properly under all conditions and Adam's life exemplifies this opinion. He is "no Sir Charles Grandison of the class to which he belongs, but an example of a high-souled working man, who has taught himself the duty of self-sacrifice." [5])

Sir Leslie Stephen observes that "Adam Bede is a most admirable portrait" and that "he corresponds to the view, which an intelligent daughter takes of a respected father," [6]) but the novelist denies this persistently : "Adam is not my father any more than Dinah is my aunt." [7]) In a letter to the Brays she acknowledged : "that there are things in it about my father (i. e.

---

[1]) *Cambridge History* XIII, p. 391.
[2]) G. Eliot, *Adam Bede*, p. 579.
[3]) Th. Carlyle, *Sartor Resartus*, p. 174.
[4]) M. L. Cazamian, *Le Roman et les Idées en Angleterre*, Ch. II, p. 113.
[5]) *Cambridge History* XIII, p. 390.
[6]) Leslie Stephen, *George Eliot*, Engl. Men of Letters, Ch. V, p. 75.
[7]) J. W. Cross, *George Eliot's Life, as related in her Letters and Journals*, Vol. II, p. 67/68.

being interpreted things, my father told us about his life)." [1])

He is the hero of self-renunciation. Just as Rochester is Charlotte Brontë's embodiment of the ideal man, the representation of masculine strength, in whom a young woman, dependent and lacking self-confidence, puts her full trust, so is Adam Bede the hero of George Eliot's dreams : a strong, trustworthy, reliable person who, with great energy, tries to do his daily task in spite of repeated oppressing sorrows which might have thrust a less energetic person out of his course, and have made him dejected, idle, and losing in courage to brave the beats of Fate. A man like Adam Bede sets an example by his conception of duty and must call forth admiration and imitation in the world. Sir Leslie Stephen is quite right in his opinion that Adam Bede is "a thorough man." [2])

The treasures of memory which afforded the authoress material for her heroes, were soon exhausted. All the heroes of the first period are based on experiences of her youth ; her later years seem not to have furnished any material. The heroes of her second period show that George Eliot "in commonplace men and manners is losing her interest ; the eye that has looked outward quite as much as inward, is now concentrated on mental and moral facts, and out of herself she creates characters to illustrate her psychological discernments." [3]) "George Eliot partit de son milieu, de ses souvenirs, de sa jeunesse, pour arriver aux problèmes sociaux, moraux, historiques," [4]) André Chevalley observes. The effect of her philosophic studies is henceforth distinctly to be traced. Her 'marriage' to G. H. Lewes called forth a storm of disapproval and caused the loss of the greater number of her friends. This abandonment for a deed which did not really affect her reputation for nobility of mind, but which the British Public simply could not condone, had forced her to a rather lonely life with only a few faithful friends for intercourse.

---
[1]) Letter from G. Eliot to the Brays, end of June 1859.
[2]) Leslie Stephen, *Hours in a Library*, Ch. III, p. 221.
[3]) W. L. Cross, *Development of the English Novel*, p. 243.
[4]) A. Chevalley, *Le Roman Anglais de notre Temps*, p. 51.

What little time was left her from her household-duties she devoted to study. The heroes of her later novels bear ample testimony to her intellectual development and to her wish to record and interpret. H. Walker states that : "no one before her time had so combined profound culture in philosophy with insight into character and keen observation." [1])

Charles Bray had seen at an early date that her heart had little to do with her observation and that it was chiefly her mind that was at work. Hence his opinion : "her sense of character of men and things is a predominatingly intellectual one, with which the Feelings have little to do." [2]) Her heroes of her first period contradict this opinion and give ample illustration of her sympathy with her fellow-creatures whom she pictures with love and with tenderness of heart. Later on her sheltered life of ease and comfort did not enable her to be a witness of or to come in contact with living examples of misery and degradation. Hence her building-up of heroes to fit pet theories. In her urgent desire to interpret characters that apparently give the impression of being out-of-the-common, and in her fervour to rouse interest for her doctrines, she overshot the mark so that the reader loses all his interest in the heroes because of the exaggerated exposure of their vices and virtues. In her later works there is "too much theory and too little observation, too much reasoning and too little intuition," [3]) which Edmund Gosse rightly ascribes to her being "weak in that quality, which more than any other is needed by a novelist : 'imaginative invention'." [4])

The sum total of vice is embodied in the hero of *Romola*, Tito Melema, "le chef-d'oeuvre du talent psychologique de George Eliot." [5]) Tito was a shipwrecked Greek, "aged twenty-three, with a dark, beautiful face, long dark curls, the brightest smile, and a

---

[1]) H. Walker, *The Literature of the Victorian Era*, p. 735.
[2]) Charles Bray, *Phases of Opinion and Experience during a long Life*, p 75.
[3]) H. Walker, *The Literature of the Victorian Era*, p. 732.
[4]) E. Gosse, *Modern English Writers*, p. 372.
[5]) E. Montégut, *Ecrivains modernes de l'Angleterre*, p. 136.

large onyx ring on his forefinger." [1]) The impression he made, however, was not so favourable, for a painter at a barber's shop wanted him to sit for the traitor Simon, for which image he tried to find a model. Of his character we read that "he could never find it easy to face displeasure and anger; ....he was not tormented by sentimental scruples," [2]) which he proved by the sale of the gems with the exception of the onyx-ring entrusted to him by his foster-father. Through the jewels he became acquainted with the scholar Bardi, a high-principled man, to whom he behaved "with a modesty which was not false, though he was conscious that it was politic." [3]) By his attractive manners he won the love of Bardi's only daughter.

One day he received a letter from his foster-father who had likewise been shipwrecked and in this way had got separated from Tito. Baldassarre Calvo implored his foster-son to find him, but Tito decided to ignore the letter. Instead of using the money obtained by the sale of the jewels for the saving of his benefactor who was the rightful owner of the gems, he kept the money for himself. Thus "he had avowed to himself a choice which he would have been ashamed to avow to others, and which would have made him ashamed in the resurgent presence of his father." [4]) Rightly George Eliot remarks, with regard to Tito's sacrificing to his egoism a man who had rescued him from a miserable life of poverty and bestowed on him all his love, that: "the inward shame, the reflex of that outward law which the great heart of mankind makes for every individual man..., that inward shame was showing its blushes in Tito's determined assertion to himself that his father was dead, or that at least search was hopeless." [5]) His future father-in-law brought him in contact with other scholars and so Tito had taken the first step on the road to a leading position among the Florentines "by meritorious exertion, by ingenious learning, by amiable

---

[1]) G. Eliot, *Romola,* Seaside Library ed., p. 75.
[2]) ibid., p. 186.   [3]) ibid., p. 41.   [4]) ibid., p. 67.   [5]) ibid., p. 67.

compliance." [1]) On the day he came to Florence a girl in the market gave him a piece of bread. He met her again on the occasion of a fair, where he married her through a mimic ceremony, and left her in the supposition that she was his wedded wife. He then shrank from causing her momentary pain, not heeding that by this weakness he committed a much greater wrong. On this G. Eliot comments: "Our deeds are like children that are born to us; they live and act apart from our own will. Nay, children may be strangled, but deeds never; they have an indestructible life both in and out of our consciousness." [2])

The first wicked deed left behind an impression that smoothed the path for further crimes. He was in need of money and sold the onyx-ring, the last of the gems entrusted to him by his father, for "he wanted now to be free from any hidden shackles that would gall him, though ever so little, under his ties to Romola." [3]) One day French prisoners were led into Florence, then at war with France. One of them seized him by the arm and he stood face to face with his foster-father. "The two men looked at each other, silent as death." [4]) Now he advanced on the path of crime by declaring his father to be "some madman." [5]) The authoress pronounces her opinion on this deed in these words: "there are moments when our passions speak and decide for us.... They carry in them an inspiration of crime, that in one instant does the work of long premeditation." [6]) He strayed farther from the path of duty and honour, for now "the only strength he trusted to lay in his ingenuity and his dissimulation" and "he hoped to be prepared for all emergencies by cool deceit — and defensive amor" [7]); he felt "as if a serpent had begun to coil round his limbs." [8]) Well he knew that his father would avenge this insult; he bought an armor and invented schemes to evade danger. Though he had promised his father-in-law never to sell the collection of books and antiques, which the old man had destined for 'an everlasting possession' to

---

[1]) ibid., p. 78.   [2]) ibid., p. 109.   [3]) ibid., p. 123.   [4]) ibid., p. 148.
[5]) ibid., p. 148. [6]) ibid., p. 148.   [7]) ibid., p. 150.   [8]) ibid., p. 149.

his fellow-citizens and which was to bear his name, he broke his promise in his need of money, forfeiting his wife's confidence and love by doing so. Until this time he had been very prosperous in his political affairs. The citizens of Florence still considered that "this ingenious and serviceable Greek was in future rather to be used for public needs." [1]) Gradually his wife and the Florentines learnt to see his real character. He was aware of this and attempted to leave Florence, deserting his legal wife whom he hated, but taking Tessa and the children with him. On the evening of his departure he found himself surrounded by armed men whom he tried to escape by jumping into the Arno. He succeeded in swimming to a safe spot where he was washed ashore exhausted just at the feet of his godfather who strangled him. "Who shall put his finger on the work of justice...." [2])

Tito's whole character is comprised in the following words: "Dans Tito, sous des dehors séduisants, se trahissent l'ingratitude égoïste, la faiblesse sensuelle, l'ambition sans scrupules, l'intrigue sans pudeur, la diplomatie dupe d'elle-même." [3]) The critic of the Westminster Review of July 1881 is quite right in his criticism of this hero, when he says: "His serpentine beauty, his winning graciousness, his aesthetic refinement, his masculine energy of intellect, his insinuating affectionateness with his selfish love of pleasure and his cowardly recoil from pain, his subdulous serenity and threacherous calm, as of a faithless summersea, make up a being that at once fascinates and repels, that invites love, but turns our love into loathing almost before we have given it." A similar judgment was given by one of the best Dutch critics who states his opinion in these words: "In zijn streven naar het veroveren eener aangename en winstgevende, voor zijn eerzucht vleijende maatschappelijke stelling ; in zijn vlieden van al hetgeen zijn rust zou kunnen verstoren of hem smartelijk zou kunnen aandoen, zien wij Tito zonder dat hij tot hiertoe in het oog der wereld zich aan één enkele misdaad

---

[1]) ibid., p. 320.   [2]) ibid., p 371.
[3]) *Revue des Deux Mondes*, Dec., 1863.

schuldig maakte, langzamerhand alle gevoelens uitschudden, die het manlijk charakter tot sieraad strekken." [1])

This exceedingly treacherous character, hidden behind a handsome face and attractive manners, is pictured by George Eliot as a study of moral decay, "gradually succumbing to the corroding effect of self-indulgence, and falling lower and lower in the moral plane, while materially he prospers marvellously." [2]) Tito is the personification of the vice which the authoress hated and detested most of all : egoism. The story of his life exactly represents the contrary of her preaching on the annulment of self. His fosterfather, being disappointed in his wife, has been too indulgent with him in the hope of being rewarded by this child's love. Tito's selfishness, instead of being checked, is fed by this indulgence and he grows up a being that only aims at his own ease, comfort and well-being, while he neglects his filial and matrimonial duties to attain this end. In spite of his attempts at evading human vengeance, he cannot escape the divine punishment which the novelist pictured as a retribution for an accumulation of offenses against God's most sacred laws. "The effects of selfishness and personal self-seeking have nowhere been so wonderfully studied by George Eliot as in this character."[3])

The story of Tito's life cannot help having its effect ; yet this accumulation of sins makes the impression of the author's wishing to force the truth home too much, that an insignificant deed can lead to an absolute moral degradation. It is a proof of her words that "we cannot foretell the working of the smallest event in our own lot." [4]) The authoress has kept up Tito's character to perfection ; she has built up this hero entirely in her mind, but whether English literature owes him to intellectual development or to intuition is difficult to decide. It is a fact that she pictured this inferior creature in a manner which betrays the extent of her psychological insight. The deterioration

---

[1]) Ch. Busken Huet, *Litterarische Fantasien en Kritieken*, 8st deel, p. 118.
[2]) E. S. Haldane, *George Eliot and her Times*, p. 207.
[3]) G. Willis Cooke, *George Eliot*, a critical Study of her Life, p. 322.
[4]) G. Eliot, *Scenes of Clerical Life*, p. 394.

of the this hero's character, which is felt from the first, is traced with almost unswerving logic. In spite of Leslie Stephen's assertion that "Tito is thoroughly and to his finger's ends a woman"[1]) his misdeeds are drawn so skilfully, that if the sex of the author were unknown, many critics would be at a loss to decide whether the authorship is due to a man or to a woman. However, it is to a woman that we owe "this elaborate study of moral deterioration under repeated shocks of tempation."[2])

Several authors, male and female, had already pronounced their opinions on existing discords and troubles and given the solution of the problems through their heroes. George Eliot also saw in a political hero a means of proclaiming her views, though Mr. J. W. Cross wrote in his wife's diary: "Party measures and party men afforded her no great interest. Representative government by numerical majorities did not appeal to her as the last word of political wisdom. Generally speaking she had little patience with talk about practical politics, which seemed to her under our present system to be often too very unpractically handled by ignorant amateurs."[3]) Her old friend, Mr. Bray, said of her: "the exceeding fairness for which she is noted towards all parties, towards all sects and denominations, is probably owing to her little feeling on the subject — at least not enough to interfere with her judgment."[4])

In spite of her indifference to politics, George Eliot tried her hand at a political novel of which Felix Holt is the hero. He is intended to represent the personification of her ideal of the real democrat by outward appearance as well as by inner conviction. He was a shaggy-headed, large-eyed, strong-limbed person[5]) in the twenty-sixth year of his life.[6]) He had been a student at Glasgow where he became acquainted with

---

[1]) Leslie Stephen, George Eliot, p. 139.
[2]) W. H. Hudson, An Introduction to the Study of Literature, p. 196.
[3]) J. W. Cross, George Eliot's Life as related in her Letters and Journals, Vol. III, p. 426/427.
[4]) Ch. Bray, Phases of Opinion and Experience during a long Life, p. 75.
[5]) G. Eliot, Felix Holt, Everyman's library, p. 55.
[6]) ibid., p. 265.

radicalism and saw poverty from very near. Owing to this he had a great disdain for the higher classes of society. By sacrificing a life free from care, because he did not want to sell a quack medicine, he acted in accordance with his openly-professed principles. (He preferred a poor, but honest existence as a watchmaker among workers like himself.) "I'll take no employment that obliges me to prop up my chin with a high cravat, and wear straps, and pass the live-long day with a set of fellows, who spend their spare money on shirt-pins. My father was a weaver first of all. It would have been better for him, if he had remained a weaver... I mean to stick to the class I belong to — people who don't follow the fashions." [1]) "I have the blood of a line of handicraftsmen in my veins and I want to stand up for the lot of the handicraftsmen, as a good lot." [2]) His only wish was to promote other people's happiness and if he could succeed in this, he thought life worth living, for "life is worth having to a man who has some sparks of sense and feeling and bravery in him. And the finest fellow would be the one who could be glad to have lived because the world was chiefly miserable, and his life had come to help some one who needed it. He would be the man who had the most powers and the fewest selfish wants." [3]) Failure of anything, undertaken for the benefit of others, was out of the question for him; it depended only on people sticking to their good intentions, for, "the only failure a man ought to fear is failure in cleaving to the purpose he sees to be the best."[4]) "Where great things can't happen, I care for very small things, such as will never be known beyond a few garrets and workshops. And then, as to one thing I believe in, I don't think I can altogether fail." [5])

The Reform Bill drew him into politics. He had not the slightest confidence in the reform of the existing polity. One thing he considered necessary for the people : education and, to promote this, the establishment of a loan-library. George Eliot proves again to be Carlyle's disciple who also expressed this in his Inaugural

---

[1]) ibid., p. 58.   [2]) ibid., p. 245.   [3]) ibid., p. 241.   [4]) ibid., p. 401.
[5]) ibid., p. 402.

speech at Edinburgh on 2nd April 1866 in the words: "The true University of our days is a collection of books.... The main use of the university is at present: a great library of good books to study and to read."

Incited to speaking by the oration of the radical's agent he proclaimed George Eliot's ideas in his speech on the nomination-day: "All the schemes about voting, and districts, and annual parliaments, and the rest, are engines, and the water or steam — the force that is to work them — must come out of human nature — out of men's passions, feelings, desires. Whether the engines will do good work or bad depends on these feelings.... I'll tell you what's the greatest power under heaven, and that is public opinion — the ruling belief in society about what is right and what is wrong, what is honourable and what is shameful...." [1])

He became acquainted with the daughter of the minister of a dissenting sect, whom he disliked for her ladylike manners and therefore treated very rudely. He expressed his dislike most insolently in: "I should like to come and scold her every day and make her cry and cut her fine hair off." [2]) Though she was very much hurt by his rude behaviour, she could not help being influenced by his opinions and ideas. He was so much her superior that she came to a longing for the strength of higher motives, whilst the beauty of his character drew her more and more to him. In the end she rejected a proposal made by a rich gentleman, that she might become the poor watchmaker's wife.

G. Willis Cooke declares the hero's personality to be: "George Eliot's ideal workman, a man who remains true to his class, seeks his own moral elevation, does not have much faith in the ballot, and who is zealous for the education of his fellows." [3]) Most readers will agree that the authoress succeeds very well in picturing the staunchness of her hero's character. Even in his love-affair he remains the same and does not sacrifice any of his principles in order to win the girl who belongs to another

---

[1]) ibid., p. 273/274.   [2]) ibid., p. 66.
[3]) G. Willis Cooke, G. *Eliot,* A critical Study of her Life, p. 325.

and higher class of society. His firm determination to devote himself to the cause of the workman, the way in which he lives up to his ideas, his dwelling in a working-quarter of the town and his bold refusal to sell the quack-medicine by which his father had made a fortune for the simple reason that it would be deceiving others, all this is bound to make an impression on her. That "the political philosophy of Felix Holt has not very much to do with the story, except as part and parcel of his manliness of character" [1]) is true. He is not a political hero in spite of the novelist's efforts to represent him as an advocate of radicalism.

Sir Leslie Stephen would like to see in him "the thoroughgoing radical, stung to fury by pauperism and the slavery of children in factories" [2]) and he ascribes the absence of this fury to "the want of masculine fibre in George Eliot and the deficient sympathy with rough popular passions." [3]) We had better be content to believe that the authoress used this hero to proclaim her opinion on the improvement of mankind, which is not to be realized by words and speeches and harangues, but by setting an example. A similar thought had occupied Carlyle's mind, which this author expressed thus: "the only solid, though a far slower reformation, is what each begins and perfects on himself." [4])

George Eliot was not interested in politics. She was "more interested in the advances of scientific thought than in the reforming energics of Gladstone's first government." [5]) Her aim was "to teach the world that true social reform is not to be secured by act of Parliament, or by the possession of the ballot on the part of all workingmen." [6]) She felt the discord in her native country but saw improvement only in improvement of the inner man.

The last of George Eliot's heroes that must come up for

---

[1]) *Cambridge History* XIII, p. 397.
[2]) Leslie Stephen, *George Eliot*, English Men of Letters, p. 155.
[3]) ibid., note 1.
[4]) Th. Carlyle, *Signs of the Time*, Critical and Miscellaneous Essays, p. 118.
[5]) Leslie Stephen, *George Eliot*, English Men of Letters, p. 199.
[6]) G. Willis Cooke, *George Eliot*, a critical Study of her Life, p. 327.

discussion is Daniel Deronda, the opposite of Tito Melema. He might be called the sum total of virtue, of all that is noble, disinterested and great in man. He represents the Sir Charles Grandison of the novels of almost a century ago. Yet an accumulation of vices presented in Tito is more natural and holds the attention of the reading public longer than a personification of perfection.

Deronda's person made a pleasant impression. He had "a seraphic face, with a pale-brown skin, a perpendicular brow, and calmly penetrating eyes,"[1] eyes "of a dark yet mild intensity, which seemed to express a special interest in every one on whom he fixed them."[2] His character was very amiable. He felt for his fellow-creatures as he was "fervently democratic in his feeling for the multitude, and yet, through his affections and imagination, intensely conservative,"[3] and though he was "voracious of speculations on government and religion, yet loath to part with long-sanctioned forms."[4] At an early age he had lost his parents and was educated by Sir Hugh Mallinger who never spoke of these parents. Sir Hugh sent him to Eton and afterwards to Cambridge. In both places the boy showed a want of ambition. His ambition kept him "exceptionally aloof from conspicuous, vulgar triumph, and from other ugly forms of boyish energy,"[5] but he had "a meditative interest in learning how human miseries are wrought."[6] He felt attracted to people "in proportion to the possibility of his defending them, rescuing them, telling upon their lives with some sort of redeeming influence."[7] Hence he helped his friend Hans Meyrick pass his examination but, by sacrificing his time for him, he failed himself. However, he was glad of the result.

When rowing on the Thames one day, he saved a Jewish girl, Mizah Cohen or Lapidoth, who wanted to drown herself. He asked Hans's mother to take her into her house, whilst he

---

[1] G. Eliot, *Daniel Deronda*, Tauchnitz ed., Vol. I, p. 271/273.
[2] ibid., Vol. II, p. 188.　　[3] ibid., p. 238.
[4] ibid., Vol. II, p. 238.　　[5] ibid., Vol. I, p. 261.　　[6] ibid., p. 261.
[7] ibid., Vol. II, p. 177.

procured the money for her board and lodging and acted as her guardian. On a journey abroad he saw a lady at the gambling-table. She lost much money and he saw her enter a pawnbroker's shop the next day. He redeemed her pawn and restored the necklace to her. He met this lady, Gwendolen Harlow, in England when she was married to a man she had taken for the sake of his money. She was very unhappy and turned to Daniel for support. The only comfort he could give her in her misery was to advise her to find an escape for her troubles in religion : "The refuge you are needing from personal trouble is the higher, the religious life, which holds an enthusiasm for something more than our own appetites and vanities. The few may find themselves in it simply by an elevation of feeling; but for us who have to struggle for our wisdom, the higher life must be a region in which the affections are clad with knowledge." [1]) In putting these words in her hero's mouth, George Eliot expresses her opinion about the value of anything whatever that attracts our attention to something outside ourselves. She points out the importance of religion, not the religion that has "faith in a personal God and in personal immortality, but that which is based on the mystery of life and nature, impressed on the sensitive soul of man in fears, sorrows, hopes, aspirations, and built up into great ideals and institutions through tradition." [2]) Deronda had not "set about one function in particular with zeal and steadiness." [3]) He attributed this to his birth, which "had laid no special demands on him." [4]) His whole life he had been conscious of a mystery hanging over his birth and he had been longing for his unknown parents.

The turning point in his life came when he heard that his mother was alive. He longed for her with "the tender yearning after a being whose life might have been the worse for not having his care and love." [5]) When he met her he experienced the sad

---

[1]) ibid., Vol. III, p. 80.
[2]) G. Willis Cooke, *George Eliot,* a critical Study of her Life, p. 338.
[3]) George Eliot, *Daniel Deronda,* Vol. IV, p. 241.
[4]) ibid., p. 240.   [5]) ibid., p. 8.

disappointment that she was not longing for her child. From her he learned that he was a Jew. His mother had always tried to conceal her descent, but Daniel was very proud of belonging to a race that had been disdained and crushed from times immemorial. He had always had a fervent craving after an ideal he could live up to and so put an end to his dilettantism and vague longing for an aim. The Jews had already drawn his attention for a long time and by his attempts to find out Mirah's relations he often came in close contact with them. He wanted to devote the rest of his life to their cause. Already a long time he had been in love with Mirah, but he did not want to propose to her for fear of being accepted out of gratitude. It turned out that Mirah was also in love with him because of his lofty, noble character. Together they wanted to go to the East, for Daniel was possessed with the noble idea of restoring : "a political existence to my people, making them a nation again, giving them a national centre, such as the English have, though they too are scattered over the surface of the globe. That is a task that presents itself to me as a duty : I am resolved to begin it, however feebly. I am resolved to devote my life to it. At the least, I may awaken a movement in other minds, such as has been awakened in my own." [1]

Daniel Deronda is the image of the hero, who is "un personage selon le coeur de George Eliot et en tout le contrepartie parfaite du Tito Melema."[2] With great skill Daniel's development in finding a mission for himself is described. His bird, as we said, "laid no demands on him... he had fallen into a meditative numbness, and was gliding farther and farther from that life of practically energetic sentiment, which he would have proclaimed to be the best of all life." [3] His "early awakened sensibility and reflectiveness had developed into a many-sided sympathy, which threatened to hinder any persistent course of action." [4] These

---

[1] ibid. p. 276/277.
[2] E. Montégut, *Ecrivains modernes de l'Angleterre*, p. 171.
[3] George Eliot, Daniel Deronda, Vol. II, p. 240.
[4] ibid., p. 238.

quotations speak sufficiently for his character and his mind, which was quite willing to defend enthusiastically the cause of the race to which he, though unknowingly, belonged. The discovery of his being a Jew gave him a task that he enthusiastically took upon him. For this social captainship, in which Busken Huet saw "de gelukkige omschrijving van een romantisch heldenkarakter," [1]) and for its aim, which he henceforth strove after, he was willing to sacrifice everything.

It will be admitted that Leslie Stephen is right, when he remarks that "D. Deronda would have embodied her [George Eliot's] sentiments more completely, if instead of devoting himself to the Jews, he had become a leading prophet in the church of humanity." [2])

Daniel Deronda with all his virtues, his sensitiveness and scruples bears a striking resemblance to the prototype of the first lady-novelists, Sir Charles Grandison. He is the worst of George Eliot's heroes, a personification of her theory on heredity. About this Leslie Stephen rightly observes: "So far as Daniel Deronda is an aesthetic embodiment of an ethical revelation — a judicious hint to a young man in search of an ideal — he represents an untenable theory." [2]) No more does Professor Saintsbury's opinion do credit to the novelist's conception: "Daniel Deronda is a parochial and grotesque idea having thoroughly mastered the writer." [3])

That he is unnatural the great many commentaries prove which the novelist thought it necessary to give to motivate this hero's deeds. On no other of her heroes does she comment so much, which is the best proof of his lack of reality.

Emile Montégut suggests that the origin of Daniel Deronda may be found in some personage of *La Femme de Claude* by Dumas fils, because "dans ce drame mal accueilli George Eliot découvrait la synthèse la plus large possible de la doctrine

---

[1]) Busken Huet, *Litterarische Fantasiën en Kritieken*, Deel VIII, p. 132.
[2]) Leslie Stephen, *George Eliot*, p. 190.
[3]) G. Saintsbury, *Three Mid-Century Novelists*, p. 281.

morale qu'elle avait prêchée toute sa vie."[1]) A novel which influenced George Eliot's thoughts for certain, is Disraeli's *Tancred*, published in 1847. The hero, Tancred of Montacute, heir of a large estate and enormous wealth, went to the Holy Land to learn in that country what faith, and what truth was. He met there an Emir, Fakredeen, who dreamed of a greater Asia and saw in Tancred a useful help. At the same time he worked out a scheme for a greater Britain for his new friend. The latter, however, only saw a means to perform great things in faith and not in all sorts of intrigues which Fakredeen proposed.

A hero like Tancred was the personification of George Eliot's thoughts and, as her store of novelmaterial had run out long ago, she satisfied her desire to create a similar hero in Daniel Deronda who, being an imitation, proved to be a failure.

In conclusion to the investigations of George Eliot's heroes the following observations may be made. The novelist continued the method of taking her heroes from the people with whom she was thoroughly acquainted. The hero, truest to life, is Adam Bede, for whom, though she denies it, her father was the model. Hence Adam Bede is the most lifelike of her heroes; he is also the personification of her heart's ideal as regards the nobility of his character and the devotion to his work. Her heroes are very different from Mrs. Gaskell's creations. Mrs. Gaskell made them act and speak for themselves and so their characters were revealed through their conversation. George Eliot speaks herself; she gives explanations to make her hero understood by the reader. She spends whole pages on the inward struggles of the soul. We learn to know the novelist's own character from these interpretations, which are edifying as regards their contents; yet they are very tedious and diminish the reader's interest in the hero. Moreover they betray George Eliot's lack of association with people, her sacrificing individualism to altruism, and her innate want of insight.

---

[1]) E. Montégut, *Ecrivains Modernes de l'Angleterre,* Première Série, p. 170.

She gains insight into character through philosophy, through books and through interchange of thoughts with prominent scholars. The result is that she is the first authoress who 'creates' a hero ; not creating in the sense of describing, as the word was used in the foregoing chapters, but in the meaning of 'building up, piling up a character from the very beginning', the foundation being a single virtue or vice. These 'creations' are called into existence with a didactic and edifying purpose and have found no imitators. Clothed in such a 'creation', Sir Charles Grandison turns up once more, but he is a faint image of the hero so much in favour among the early novelists, only approaching this figure's perfection in his mental and moral qualities. In every life she saw at work the law of hereditary transmission and "much that enters into human life of weal and woe is to be comprehended only with reference to this law." [1]) Her heroes only serve as intermediaries through whom the novelist wants to point out that a deed committed is not a single fact, but is the result of innumerable situations and consequences, each insignificant in itself, but together and in succession often leading to a deed, which rouses general admiration or disapproval. The critic of the *Westminster Review* observed : "we have found in her teaching the enforcement of the doctrine of consequences more richly illustrated, more variously applied, more scientifically stated than ever it was before." [2])

Her heroes differ from those created up till then in having characters which are not yet formed. They grow, they develop for the better, or they sink lower and lower. However, "no great work of art, a convincing portrait of a personality, has been created by diligent thought." [3]) The reader prefers to enjoy the actions of a living hero, of a personality he can comprehend. The adventures of a being, never met with in daily life but only 'invented', must necessarily become insipid

---

[1]) G. Willis Cooke, *George Eliot*, A Critical Study of her Life, p. 167.
[2]) *Westminster Review*, July, 1881.
[3]) Harold Williams, *Modern English Writers*, p. 425.

and lose their interest. Hence Edmund Gosse's verdict: "The intellectual self-sufficiency of George Eliot has suffered severe chastisement. At the present day scanty justice is done to her unquestionable distinction of intellect or to the emotional intensity of much of her early work." [1] Nevertheless, through the heroes of her second period she takes up a unique place in English literary history; by those of her first she shares her glory with her comtemporary, Mrs. Gaskell.

---

[1] Edmund Gosse, *Modern English Writers*, p. 372.

CHAPTER XIV.

Mrs. HUMPHRY WARD (1851—1920).

The middle and the latter part of the nineteenth century was the scene of a religious revival and great political activity. The Oxford movement, which drove Newman out of the Established Church, had subsided and many people, who had first left the church, had gradually returned to it. Another more serious religious revolution made people desert all religious belief and a scepticism followed, that vented itself in writings. Darwin's *Origin of Species* published in 1859 was in itself an attack on the Church which had resisted so many attacks already, but these had come to nothing every time, because they tried to pull down the old creed without putting anything else in its place. Darwin was able to replace the worn-out dogmas by something concrete; he looked for truth and based it on experience. A few years before this Spencer's *Principles of Psychology* had explained by philosophy questions which gave rise to doubt, forming a contrast with Darwin's theories. Huxley succeeded in holding the general interest by applying science to daily life.

As a reaction against the want of religious feeling and the sceptic view of things, a vehement struggle in the church followed, which gradually subsided, but in many hearts a longing was kindled for something more realistic, less mysterious and not merely built on an acceptation of formulae. Intellectual England was striving to do away with the old dogmas and trying to find a firm basis for its religious life. The name of Matthew Arnold is closely linked with this reaction.

Certain social questions had been solved, but new ones

constantly arose and interested prominent radicals and socialists. Disraeli, when prime-minister (1874—'80), wanted to leave the social problems alone and tried to engage the people's thoughts by schemes of colonial expansion in order to secure England's pre-eminence in Europe and to offer to the English race the dictatorship of the globe.

A clever woman, Mrs. Humphry Ward, a niece of Matthew Arnold, took up a foremost place among those writers who treated these new ideas and problems. When a problem had roused her interest, she examined and discussed it beforehand with persons who could give her all the information she wanted. The outcome of these discussions she turned into a novel, the hero of which suggested a solution to the problem.

The author's life offers a striking contrast to the lives of the novelists already discussed, which perhaps accounts in no small degree for the conception of her heroes.

Mary Arnold was born at Hobart Town in Tasmania on June 11th 1851. Her father, having turned Roman-Catholic was compelled to leave the colony in 1856. He went to England and worked under Newman at the Roman-Catholic university of Dublin, and later at the Birmingham Oratory, till, in 1864, he turned against Catholicism. Then he established himself with his family at Oxford. Here Mary spent her life till her marriage to the well-known art-critic Humphry Ward.

She came in contact with prominent intellectual people like Jowett, Pusey, Thomas Hill Green, the great historian, (who was to be Mr. Grey in *Robert Elsmere)* and Mark Pattison, one of the greatest scholars of Europe and a sceptic in religious matters. From childhood she had heard of religious disputes and philosophical questions. A few years before her marriage she had begun studying early Spanish literature, in which she was so well-read, that the above-mentioned Mr. Green recommended her as the best person for writing a book on Spain. Through these studies of Spain and the Spaniards she had grown interested in the origins of Christianity. Through her investigations into Christian documents, she concluded that the greater part of the New Testament must have been the product of a period of strong belief in miracles, and that the interpretation of the Bible was only a series of obsolete form that failed to convince and hold the people. In 1873 she wrote to her father: "Just now it seems to me that one cannot make one's belief too simple or hold what one does believe too strongly. Of dogmatic Christianity I can make nothing. Nothing is clear except the personal character of Christ and that view of Him as the founder and lawgiver of a new society which struck me years ago in Ecce Homo. And the more I read and think over the New Testament the more impossible it seems to me to accept what is ordinarily called the scheme of Christianity." She wished that the original message of Christianity should be known and revered, freed from dogmas, stripped of every disguise and that its truth might be understood by everybody. To Mrs. Edward Conybeare she wrote: "The more I think and read the more plain the great lines of that distant part become to me, the more dearly I see God at work there, through the forms of thought, the beliefs, the capacities of the first three centuries, as I see Him at work now, through the form of thought, the beliefs and the capacities of our own."[1] She clearly saw that the Anglican church could no longer satisfy the average Englishman with his inclination for examining his religion and his Bible with its mysteries. If the church was to remain the church of the nation, if it was to keep its members together, she saw a solution of the problem only in depriving the creed of its symbols and dogmas. She revolted against Anglican orthodoxy and arrogance and its attempt to coerce people who could not possibly care for religion in its present disguise. At that time she was of opinion that, if one did not believe in the creed any longer, one should leave the church. Belonging to the Anglican church herself she had the boldness to stand up for her conviction. The adherents of the new theory were small in number, for the majority of churchgoers

---

[1] Letter from Mrs. H. Ward to Mrs. Edward Conybeare, May 16th, 1888.

still clung to the worship of God in its existing form. Mrs. Ward was a disciple of her Uncle Matthew Arnold who expressed his opinion that the one thing necessary was 'to find for the Bible, for Christianity, for our religion a basis in something which can be verified instead of in something which has to be assumed. This must be the first business. With his problem unsolved, all other religious discussion is idle trifling.'

In her first novel *Robert Elsmere*, published in 1888, she expressed her views of religious matters, and also carried out her imperialistic doctrines on a moderate scale (Till the end of her life she was an advocate of imperialism). The hero of one of her other novels reveals to the full her ideas with regard to this.

Robert Elsmere, with whom she opened her series of heroes, was not attractive as far as outward appearance is concerned. He had "a large mouth, bright reddish hair and quick grey eyes, while his figure was tall and loosely joined; the shoulders were narrow, the arms inordinately long and the extremities too small for the general height." [1] The heroine liked him from the beginning for his eager face. "Eagerness seemed to be the note of the whole man, of the quick eyes and mouth, the flexible hands and energetic movements." [2] She felt attracted to him when they were talking about "the large things of life", for then in his eyes "shone a beautiful, mystical light, responsive, lofty, full of soul." [3] He was educated at Oxford where his tutor Langham, a sceptic scholar, was the first who exercised great influence upon him. Then he heard Mr. Grey, a professor of moral philosophy, deliver a lay-sermon. He came under his influence, which made him "a man of ardour and conviction." [4] Professor Grey, "for whom God, consciousness and duty were the only realities," [5] had given up the church because he did not believe in miracles. Robert entered the church more from enthusiasm than from conviction and admiration for the

---

[1] Mrs. Humphry Ward, *Robert Elsmere*, Nelson ed., p. 25.
[2] ibid., p. 38.   [3] ibid., p. 40.   [4] ibid., p. 63.   [5] ibid., p. 64.

sacramental ceremonies of the church. However, "to the English Church as a great national institution for the promotion of God's work on earth no one could have been more deeply loyal." [1] After getting the living of Murewell and marrying a High-Church woman, he came into contact with the Squire, Roger Wendower, a disciple of Newman, who possessed one of the finest libraries in the world. This man was greatly interested in the human problems which were the underlying motives of history, and had written two well-known books. Robert also took great interest in history and was encouraged in his studies by the squire who put his entire library at his disposal. (The authoress had also learnt to see into the problems of Christianity through her own historical studies). Through Robert's discussions with the squire on religious subjects, his study of history, his reading Darwin's *Origin of Species*, and his own reflections on the Two Testaments "a whole new mental picture rose up before him, effacing, pushing out innumerable older images of thought. It was the image of a purely human Christ — a purely human, explicable, yet always wonderful Christianity." [2] He was sure, after examining himself, that he believed in God, but that he no longer believed in miracles. "I can believe no longer in an Incarnation and Resurrection. Christ is risen in our hearts, in the Christian life of charity. Miracle is a natural product of human feeling and imagination; and God was in Jesus.... not otherwise in kind than He is in me or you." [3] This is exactly what Matthew Arnold proclaimed in his *Literature and Dogma* published in 1873 : 'Miracles do not happen.' Robert felt that he could no longer be a minister in the Church of England, though the Squire advised him to do so. In this Mrs. Ward differed in opinion from a number of liberal clergymen "for whom the old letter of inspiration no longer existed, though they stoutly maintained their orthodoxy as members and ministers of the Church of England." [4] Elsmere knew that it

---

[1] ibid., p. 70. [2] ibid., p. 314. [3] ibid., p. 353.
[4] G. M. Trevelyan, *The Life of Mrs. Humphry Ward*, p. 17.

would cause his wife much pain, but he could not continue a life of deceit, preaching every Sunday things which he could not believe himself. At length he told his wife who besought him to wait a little before sending in his resignation, hoping he might go back on his decision. He gave in, but said: 'It is not that I think differently of this point or that point — but of life and religion altogether. I see God's purpose in quite other proportions as it were. Christianity seems to me something small and local. Behind it, around it — including it — I see the great drama of the world, sweeping on — led by God — from change to change, from act to act. It is not that Christianity is false, but that it is only an imperfect human reflection of a part of truth. Truth has never been, can never be, contained in any one creed or system!" [1]) He felt strengthened by his new faith and was sure he should find the means to lead a life, happier and without doubts. Full of plans and faith in God, he established himself in the poor lastern part of London. There he became acquainted with a great number of men like himself, who wanted "to gain a new social bond, a new compelling force in man and in society." [2]) This idea was put into practice by devoting their leisure to improving the state of the poor in that district. They established 'The New Brotherhood' which still continued after Robert's death, proving that the real spirit of God was in it and worked through it.

With great spiritual insight Mrs. Ward shows her readers "the struggle of a soul in its voyage towards newer theistic aspirations after losing the landmarks of the old faith." [3]) To her son-in-law she wrote on Easter Day 1910: "I more and more believe that the whole resurrection story arose from the transference of the body by the Romans.... The vacant grave seems to me a historical fact.... perhaps springing from 'one' vivid dream of a disciple.... and then theology and poetry,

---

[1]) Mrs. Humphry Ward, *Robert Elsmere*, Nelson's ed., p. 355.
[2]) ibid., p. 548.
[3]) *Chambers's Cyclopaedia of English literature*, Vol. III.

environment and inherited belief did the rest." The Church, according to Mrs. Ward should do away with these formulae which had lost vitality and put something in their places that was more in keeping with the spirit of the period. The institution of the New Brotherhood was the foundation of a new church, "of a simple and commemorative form of Christianity," [1]) which is the religious conception of the Lord's message for that time or age, the manifestation of what subconsciously sleeps in the hearts of a whole generation, a Christianity entirely human. Every age has its own version, its own interpretation, they are "the Vestures, under which men at various periods embodied and represented for themselves the religious Principle ; — invested the Divine Idea of the world with a sensible and practically active Body, so that it might dwell among them as a living and a life-giving World." [2])

J. Stuart Walters rightly states that : "Elsmere stands for a creed of no mere arid Unitarianism, but for a religion of action — a blessed blend of all that is best in Christianity with much that is good in the ideals of Marx and Spencer." [3]) Mr. Firmin Roz is the spokesman of Mrs. Ward's own sentiments when he says : "Robert Elsmere est un idéal, qui doit être l'idéal de son pays et de son race." [4])

Mrs. Ward made her hero die a martyr for the great cause, just like so many that went before him, whose works still live and are continued, for he was for her "a link in the chain of liberators of all ages." [5]) She felt that a clergyman like Elsmere could not succeed as a pastor, when he did not himself believe the words which he spoke to his congregation. The only escape from this difficult position the novelist saw in a union of equally-minded people who could form a new community and hold a

---

[1]) Mrs. Humphry Ward, *Richard Meynell*, p. 15.
[2]) Th. Carlyle, *Sartor Resartus*, Collins' Classics, p. 190.
[3]) J. Stuart Walters, *Mrs. Humphry Ward, Her Work and Influence*, p. 84.
[4]) *Revue des Deux Mondes*, 15 Mars 1910.
[5]) G. M. Trevelyan, *The Life of Mrs. Humphry Ward*, p. 50.

faith freed from all that mankind had woven round it in the course of centuries.

This hero of modernism was a faultless man, an enthusiast who, without any internal conflict, any far-going scientific investigations into the existing belief, accepted what more enlightened minds had learned to see. Their conception of conditions in the Church was transferred to him. The novelist too often gives an explanation of the difficulties which the hero has to encounter and to solve, instead of letting him speak for himself in conversation with others. This makes the hero less natural. He cared for his parishioners and their welfare not only as a spiritual, but as a real father. This care is a characteristic feature of the imperialist whose first duty was the condition of his fellow-men.

It is no wonder that the hero created a sensation. His endeavours to see the original message of Christianity, his making himself free by deserting his clerical orders, by refashioning the church of Christ as a human ideal, all this interested most readers, as it was a process, that in various disguises, occupied most of them or was going on around them. "Robert Elsmere, the doubting clergyman, was a familiar figure during the decade 1890—1900." [1]

In the sequel to this novel, *The Case of Richard Meynell*, published fifteen years afterwards, the hero was a much stronger personality, a far higher and more energetic type than Robert Elsmere. During this time the world of thought had moved rapidly. Modernism had fully set in and claimed a right for its followers in the Anglican Church which was gradually losing its hold on a great number of its members, because the interpretation of the creed did not satisfy them any longer. The person of the hero, Richard Meynell, the rector of Upcote Minor, a mining village in the Midlands, was very attractive. He was a man of "remarkable vigour, physical and mental," with "a massive head covered with strong black hair, curly at the brows, eyes

---

[1] J. Stuart Walters, *Mrs. Humphry Ward, Her Work and Influence,* Ch. V, p. 193.

greyish blue, small with some shades of expression in them which made them arresting, commanding even; a large nose and irregular mouth, the lips flexible and kind, the chin firm.... and a broad-chested, loose-limbed frame. The hands were those of a man of letters — bony and long-fingered, but refined." [1] His parents died while he was yet young, leaving him to bring up his two brothers. At the time of this story he lived with a housekeeper, who "spent hours of the night in indignantly guessing at what he [Meynell] spent on the clothes and the food of other people." [2]

He had been ordained according to the rites of the Anglican Church. However, the modern historical, critical and scientific problems had brought him "the crystallisation of doubt and passion of a freed faith." [3] Robert Elsmere felt himself forced to leave the church twenty years before this. Meantime the movement had made such rapid progress that Meynell with an exceedingly great number of priests and laiety now claimed a place in the National Church. He had always expressed himself on the necessity of including everybody in the Church, even the Dissenters. This was also one of Matthew Arnold's views which Mrs. Ward shared.

Robert Elsmere's daughter, who felt attracted to him by "his power and his transparent purity of heart" [4] took great interest in his doings. He told her all about the progress of the movement and gave her an enthusiastic description of his wishes in the words he wanted to speak to his fellow-men: "Cease from groping among ruins! — from making life and faith depend upon whether Christ was born at Bethlehem or at Nazareth, whether he rose, or did not rise, whether Luke or someone else wrote the Third Gospel, whether the Fourth Gospel is history or poetry. The life-giving force is 'here' and 'now'! It is burning in your life and mine — as it burnt in the life of Christ. Give all you have to

---

[1] Mrs. Humphry Ward, *The Case of Richard Meynell*, Smith and Elder ed., p. 9.
[2] ibid., p. 20. [3] ibid., p. 69. [4] ibid., p. 69.

the flame of it — let it consume the chaff and purify the gold. Take the cup of water to the thirsty, heal the sick, tend the dying, and feel it thrill within you — the ineffable, the immortal life! Let the false miracle go! — the true has grown out of it, up from it, as the flower from the sheath. Ah! but then we turn to the sons of tradition, and we say: "we too must have our rights in what they have built up, the past has bequeathed — as well as you! Not for you alone, the institutions, the buildings, the arts, the traditions, that the Christlife has so far fashioned for itself. They who made them are our fathers, no less than yours, — give us our share in them! — we claim it! Give us our share in the Cathedrals and Churches of our country — our share in the beauty and Majesty of our ancestral Christianity. ....Give us the rights and the citizenship that belongs to us! But do not imagine that we want to attack yours. In God's name, follow your own forms of faith, — but allow us ours also, within the common shelter of the common Church. We are children of the same God — followers of the same Master. Who made you judges and dividers over us? You shall not drive us into the desert any more. A new movement of revolt has come — an hour of upheaval — and the men with it!"[1]

The bishop of Meynell's diocese, his personal friend, because he knew the excellent qualities of his rector, asked him to account for his behaviour, and required that he should change his sermons, reminding him of the promise at his ordination. Meynell, regretting to have to inflict pain on his old friend, firmly refused to do so. He said: "I was a boy then — I am a man now. I took those vows sincerely and in absolute good faith; and all the changes in me have come about, as it seems to me, by the inbreathing of a spirit not my own — partly from our knowledge — partly in trying to help any people to live — or to die. They represent to me things lawfully — divinely — learnt.... ....I accepted certain rules and conditions. Now that I break them, must I not resign the position dependent on

---
[1] ibid., p. 72.

them? Clearly, if it were a question of any ordinary society. But the Christian church is not an ordinary society! It is the sum of Christian life! And that Life makes the Church — moulds it afresh, from age to age. There are times — we hold — when the church very nearly expresses the Life; there are others when there are great discordances between the Life, and its expression in the Church. We believe that there are such discordances now; because — once more — of a New Learning. And we believe that to withdraw from the struggle to make the Church more fully represent Life, would be sheer disloyalty and cowardice. We must stay it out and do our best...." [1]

The rector was greatly respected and esteemed in his parish. His opponents tried to find something in his personal life that might sully his reputation and through this do harm to the modernist movement. One of his enemies happened to learn a story of the life-secret of one of his female parishioners; he was said to be the father of this lady's child. His sense of honour towards the lady in question forbade him to clear himself of the accusation at her expense. Fortunately the story proved to be false. A short time afterwards the hero received another blow by the death of this child, a self-willed, obstinate creature, whom he had promised to take care of. She had gone to ruin in spite of all his efforts to keep her in the right track, but through his failure in this, he got mental scruples about being the leader of the modernist movement. Mary Elsmere, who had promised to become Meynell's wife, succeeded in convincing him that private reasons should not make him shrink from the spiritual leadership. After long thinking and after many searchings of hearts, he saw the truth of her words.

His preaching was examined in the Court of Arches, where the Dean pronounced the sentence of "depriviation ab officio et beneficio in the Church of England." [2] Meynell lodged an appeal to the Privy Council and people spoke of a Modernist petition to Parliament. Before the case was looked into in the

---

[1] ibid., p. 106.   [2] ibid., p. 500.

Privy Council the Modernists held a great gathering in Dunchester Cathedral, where Meynell delivered a sermon, afterwards known as 'The Two Christianities', "which was to be the battle-cry of the Movement, in the second part of its history." [1] The following parts of his sermon are worth mentioning, because they entirely represent Mrs. Ward's ideas of the religious movement: "My friends, what is the life either of intellect or spirit but the response of man to the communication of God ? Age by age, man's consciousness cuts deeper into the vast mystery that surrounds us ; absorbs, transmutes, translates ever more truth, into conceptions he can use, and language he can understand. From this endless process arose science — and history — and philosophy. But just as science, and history, and philosophy change with this ever-living and growing advance, so religion — man's ideas of God and his own soul...." [2]

"What is history ? Simply the power — depending upon a thousand laborious processes — of constructing a magic lens within the mind, which allows us to look deep into the past, to see its life and colour and movement again, as no generation but our own has yet been able to see it.... It has been a new and marvellous gift of our God to us ; and it has transformed or is transforming Christianity...." [3]

"There, for the Modernist, lies revelation ! — in the unfolding of the Christian idea, through the successive stages of human thought and imagination it has traversed, down to the burst of revelation in the present day. Yet we are only now at the beginning of an immense development. The content of the Christian idea of love —, love, self-renouncing, self-fulfilling — is infinite, inexhaustible, like that of beauty, or of truth. Why ? Because.... these governing ideas of our life — tested by life, confirmed by life — have their source in the very being of God, shares in His Eternity, His Ever-Fruitfulness...." [4]

This hero is a great moral force, whose enthusiasm for his cause must necessarily influence a great many doubting people.

---
[1]) ibid., p. 501. [2]) ibid., p. 517. [3]) ibid., p. 518. [4]) ibid., p. 519.

If a cause is to succeed in the end, born leaders like Meynell, an example of all that is noble in mortal man, must be the mental guides. Their way of living and acting is proof of the fight being noble. The avowal of their conviction will help to crystallise what partly consciously, partly subconsciously slumbers in the minds of their hearers.

Her solution of the problem that kept so many minds busy through the speech of this hero, drew André Chrevillon's admiration, expressed in an undated letter to the authoress: "Le problème religieux que vous posez là est vital, et la solution que vous y prévoyez dans votre pays, cette possibilité d'un christianisme évolué, adaptée, qui conserverait les formes anciennes avec leur puissance si efficace de prestige, tout en attribuant de plus en plus aux vieilles formules, aux vieux rites une valeur de symbole — cette solution est celle que l'on peut espérer du protestantisme, lequel est relativement peu cristalisé et peut encore évoluer. Même dans l'anglicanisme la part de l'interprétation personnelle a toujours été assez grande."

Mrs. Ward lost sight of the fact, however, that interest in a hero cannot be maintained by making him merely the spokesman of the author's views. In his life there is no question of mental agony, no difficulties in his love for the woman he wants for his bride, no other trouble that refers to real life.

Though Mrs. Ward was a Protestant she had the advantage of being well acquainted with the Roman-Catholic mind, her father being a Roman-Catholic with whom she used to discuss all subjects and books on Catholicism. "Catholicism has an enormous attraction for me, yet I could no more be a Catholic than a Mahometan. Only, never let us forget how much of Catholicism is based as Uncle Matt would have said, on 'Natural Truth' — truth of human nature and truth of moral experience. The visible, imperishable society — the Kingdom of Heaven in our midst — no greater idea it seems to me, was ever thrown into the world of man." These words she wrote to her son-in-law a few years after *Helbeck of Bannisdale* was published.

Her purpose in writing a novel with a rigid Roman-Catholic for its hero she explained to an ex-Catholic friend: "In my root-idea of him, Helbeck was to represent the old Catholic crossed with that more mystical and enthusiastic spirit, brought in by such converts as Ward and Faber, under Roman and Italian influence. I gather, both from books and experience, that the more fervent ideas and practices, which the old Catholics of the 'forties' disliked, have as a matter of fact, obtained a large ascendency in the present practice of Catholics, just as Ritualism has forced the hands of the older High Churchmen. And I thought one might in the matter of austerities conceive a man directly influenced by the daily reading of the Lives of the Saints and obtaining in middle life, after probation and under special circumstances as it were, leave to follow his inclinations." [1]) She wished to create in Alan Helbeck a man of whom Dr. Friedland, a Cambridge professor and friend of the heroine's father, said that he was "no mean or puerile type, with all its fetichisms and unreasons on its head — no! — a type sprung from the best English blood, disciplined by heroic memories, by the persecution and hardships of the Penal Laws." [2])

In a few words the authoress paints the hero's portrait: a stern man of about thirty-seven, remarkably tall [3]) with grey eyes, long features and a pointed chin. [4]) He was an aristocrat to his fingers' ends and the heroine's father had said that his manners and bearing were those "of a man of rank, though not of fashion." [5])

He was educated at Stone College, a Jesuit institution. For years he had wished to become a Jesuit himself, but "the obligations of his name and place had stood in the way." [6]) He was greatly attracted to his race "by a secret affection, issuing from their privations and persecutions, their faults, their dumb and

---
[1]) G. M. Trevelyan, *The Life of Mrs. Humphry Ward*, p. 147.
[2]) Mrs. Humphry Ward, *Helbeck of Bannisdale*, Smith and Elder ed., p. 367.
[3]) ibid., p. 2.   [4]) ibid., p. 14.   [5]) ibid., p. 301.   [6]) ibid., p. 256.

stupid fidelities." [1]) He finished his studies at Louvain where he spent a wretched time reading many sceptical French books.

The agonies of death of one of his masters nearly brought him to loss of faith, though "by God's grace he never gave up Confession and Communion." [2]) The administration of the last sacraments to a dying bishop and the words of the creed of Pius IV 'Sic me Deus adjuvet et Sancta Dei Evangelica' made such a deep impression upon him that he was converted again. Then he became an ascetic, devoted Roman-Catholic who "for more than twenty years by prayer and meditation, by all the ingenious means that the Catholic Church provides, had developed the sensibilities of faith.... His heart, his life were in his faith." [3]) For the benefit of the church he had remained unmarried. He had sold most of his property to establish convents and orphanages. People told that he had converted a lad of the neighbourhood who, however, declared that is was Helbeck's example that "had brought him to faith." [4]) When his widowed sister came to live with him he was not slow in coming under the influence of her stepdaughter, who openly confessed her dislike to all that was Catholic. Love came again into his life : "it was fifteen years since a woman's voice, a woman's presence, had mattered anything at all to him." [5]) Henceforward his life was divided between the divine love of God and the human love for this girl. That the course of events brought her into his life, he considered not as a "temptation, but a Divine volition concerning him." [6]) He was often tempted to sacrifice to this girl the time he was accustomed to spend on strict religious duties, but "he crushed the temptation, guided, inflamed by that profound idea of a substituted life and a vicarious obedience which has been among the root forces of Christianity." [7]) One day he rebuked Laura, the heroine, for having sown the seeds of doubt in a child. She had said that she thought the story horrible which the Sisters of the School had told, and which the child liked so much. "What

---

[1]) ibid., p. 256. [2]) ibid., p. 351. [3]) ibid., p. 138. [4]) ibid., p. 305.
[5]) ibid., p. 139. [6]) ibid., p. 297. [7]) ibid., p. 298.

has a child to do with doubt or revolt ? For her — for all of us — doubt is misery !" [1]) Through these words the novelist refers to all the misery she has witnessed in Oxford and London, resulting from the doubts of faith, to which she refers once more when Dr. Friedland said to his wife : "To doubt.... there's no harder task in the world." [2])

He promised his betrothed not to sell the Romney, a picture of his great-grandmother, his last valuable possession, of which Laura was very fond. His obligations to his orphans, however, forced him to make this sale, the only alternative being the sale of a piece of land for the building of an Anglican Church. His hatred of this Church as an institution was proved by his words : "It has been a fixed principle with me throughout my life to give no help, direct or indirect to a schismatical and rebellious church." [4])

The heroine was never certain that she should take up the first place in his life and did not get a definite answer when she sounded him on this subject. She broke off the engagement and though this was renewed when they met again at her stepmother's deathbed, she did not feel sure of him and preferred death. After she was found drowned, he became a Jesuit.

Alan Helbeck is according to J. Stuart Walters a representative of those, who keep "aflame the smouldering lamps of Catholicism in our rural districts, and by his dogged devotion helps to hold back the ever-encroaching wave of indifferentism."[5]) In this character, Mrs. Ward clearly presents the moral and intellectual depression which is the outcome of Catholicism. It is impossible to agree with the already mentioned Dr. Friedland who is of opinion that "Helbeck of Bannisdale represents Catholicism at its best." [6]) It is truer to say, at its worst. A man of nearly forty years old, in the full possession of his common sense, however devoted he may be to his church,

---

[1]) ibid., p. 130.   [2]) ibid., p. 367.   [3]) ibid., p. 288.   [4]) ibid., p. 288.
[5]) J. Stuart Walters, *Mrs. Humphry Ward, Her Work and Influence*, p. 194.
[6]) Mrs. Humphry Ward, *Helbeck of Bannisdale*, p. 367.

owes to his ancestors, to whom he is so much attached, a good management of the property they bequeathed to him. Laura saw that the Sisters, who taught the children, were ignorant, yet for the keeping up of such a school or the establishment of a similar one the precious Romney had to be sold. Helbeck was entirely in the hands of the Church which used him as a fine bird worth plucking. The Church dragged him down instead of raising him above himself, for it drove him to hate other creeds. It was the cause that the girl whom he looks upon as sent by God is forced to an untimely death. It would have been more natural, if such a fervent Roman-Catholic had considered her a temptress sent by the Most High to try his faith.

Still in his love for the Church he remained the superior, disinterested man, whom nothing could persuade to make the Church occupy the second place in his mind. For it he sacrificed all the happiness that he might expect from a union with Laura. If he had made his love for Laura his first and foremost thought he might have served the Church and its extension on earth in a far greater degree, for Laura wanted to become a Roman-Catholic. Mrs. Ward reveals through this hero, that "l'atmosphère morale et intellectuelle du Catholicisme est absolument irrespirable, désormais, pour une âme supérieure." [1] Helbeck of Bannisdale's life is "a tragedy — the struggle of two masterful energies in a man's or woman's soul — the ceaseless fight between character and circumstances," [2] and "the spiritual struggle of a devout Catholic in contact with modern unbelief." [3]

This lady novelist was interested not only in religious matters, but also in the political and social questions of her country. In her novels *Marcella* and *Sir George Tressady*, which successively appeared in 1894 and 1896, the leading social problems are treated.

In spite of efforts to cling to privileges of class and rank, the

---

[1] *Revue des Deux Mondes*, 15 Oct., 1898.
[2] W. L. Courtney, *The Feminine Note in Fiction*, p. 25.
[3] W. L. Cross, *Development of the English Novel*, p. 269.

higher classes had to give in. They grew more and more interested in social affairs and began to show this interest by taking part in social work. Parliament is of course the place where the battle between old ideas and modern views is fought most keenly. After the housing of the poor had been taken in hand by the State in 1834, everything else on behalf of the destitute was left to charitable and philanthropic institutions. Mrs. Ward's opinion was that the State should look after these things and not leave them to the good-will of private persons. Holding strong imperialistic and conservative views, she discussed and criticised social theories, at the same time giving her solution to the problem. She made great efforts to prepare herself well to handle this problem, hoping to make her influence felt in practical life. It was Mr. Sydney Buxton, a liberal friend, who gave himself infinite trouble "to pilot Mrs. Ward through the intricacies of the Parliamentary situation, required for *Sir George Tressady*." [1]) The hero of the first-named novel was a man after her own heart, a serious man of thirty, [2]) tall, with a strong build, pale but healthy aquiline face, [3]) inconspicuous brown eyes and hair. [4]) The heroine did not think him handsome, but "liked the quiet, cautious strength of his English expression and bearing." [5]) He was heir to an ancient name and to a large fortune, a true Tory "possessed by natural inheritance of the finer instincts of aristocratic rule." [6]) As a student at Cambrige he had already concerned himself with "the responsibilities of the rich, the disadvantages of the poor, the relation of the State to the individual." [7]) There he had become a close friend of Hallin, a socialist of the purest make, with whom he widely differed in opinion, but who had great influence on his political views. He was very much interested in agriculture, in economy and especially in the condition of the poor; his theories on all these themes he put into practice in a somewhat neglected part of his

---

[1]) G. M. Trevelyan, *The Life of Mrs. Humphry Ward*, Ch. VI, p. 115.
[2]) Mrs. Humphry Ward, *Marcella*, Macmillan's Novelists' Library, p. 1.
[3]) ibid., p. 46. [4]) ibid., p. 46. [5]) ibid., p. 40. [6]) ibid., p. 45.
[7]) ibid., p. 43.

grandfather's estate. He helped his grandfather in the management of the estate and was looked up to with great respect. Yet this respect did not entirely please him. Contrasted with "the great world-spectacle perpetually in his eye and thought, the small old-world pomps and feudalisms of his own existence had a way of looking ridiculous to him. He constantly felt himself absurd. It was ludicrously clear to him, for instance, that in this kingdom he had inherited it would be thought a huge condescension on his part, if he were to ask the secretary of a trades union to dine with him at the Court. Whereas, in his own honest opinion, the secretary had a far more important and interesting post in the universe than he." [1]

He fell in love with a girl who was a socialist at heart and only accepted his suit in the hope of being enabled by his large fortune to carry out her ideas. Thus he came again into contact with socialism. As yet he had, however, no faith in the government by the multitude, though he clearly saw that the times were ripe for democracy. To his great grief his fiancee broke off the engagement, when he refused to pardon a poacher who had committed a murder.

At that time he entered upon his political career, being elected conservative member of Parliament for East-Brookshire. Before the nominationday he made a speech "in praise of a progress which should go safely and wisely from step to step, and run no risks of dangerous reaction." [2] (This last sentence reflects Mrs. Ward's conservative ideas). Soon after he was made Under-Secretary of the Home Department and after his grandfather's death he took his seat in the House of Lords. By coincidence he met his former betrothed whose loss he still regretted and with whom he was still in love. She had lived and worked among the poor in London and had learned to see the truth of Aldous's opinion that changes cannot be brought about by the workman, but that a government of intellectual persons must take the lead. He, the wealthy land-owner, a member of the privileged

---

[1] ibid., p. 515.   [2] ibid., p. 187.

class, had also shown her "how wealth might be a true moral burden and test, the source of half the difficulties and pains — of half the nobleness also — of a man's life. Not in mere wealth and poverty, but in things of quite another order — things of social sympathy and relation — alterable at every turn, even under existing conditions, by the human will, lie the real barriers that divide us man from man." [1]) By his high principles he won her love. As a fruit of their united ideas he introduced into Parliament a bill of far-reaching consequences for the benefit of the working-majority.

Aldous Raeburn, the later Lord Maxwell, expresses Mrs. Humphry Ward's views on the social conditions during the last years of the 19th century. Seeing the wants of the growing democracy, feeling the need of an unavoidable change, she wants to force home her conviction that this change can only be brought about by strong-willed, noble-minded persons of high morals who have a fixed purpose before them; who, with eyes open to the future do not cast aside at once what former generations of the governing classes have attained by gradual stages and steady progress. Her hero embodies a man, "typical of the real aristocrat, true to the traditions of his race, thorough master of himself, strongly imbued with a sense of duty to his country."[2]) He is the average Englishman, a man of discipline and energy, a representative of conservatism and traditionalism, a born leader and statesman.

As the heroine is the principal person on whom the story turns the hero's ideas are only revealed when he must act as a check on the impetuous and inconsiderate girl. In Aldous Raeburn democratic ideas are continually fermenting, but are hampered by his conservative feelings. Compared with him, however, the hero of the sequel novel cuts a poor figure.

Sir George Tressady was by nature "an easy-going fellow

---

[1]) ibid., p. 542.
[2]) J. Stuart Walters, *Mrs. Humphry Ward, Her Work and Influence*, p. 80.

with no particular depth," [1]) tall, with a thin, long face, [2]) straight, fair hair, a long, pointed chin, slightly protruding," [3]) a fair moustache and a sunburnt skin." [4]) After his father's death he had gratified his longing for travelling, and having been interested in Eastern problems when at college, he had visited most parts of Asia and had written signed articles, strongly English and Imperialistic, for a leading newspaper. These articles attracted the attention of the leader of a conservative group in the House of Commons, who saw in him a promising politician. Through his influence he was elected a member of Parliament. He was a Tory to the backbone and his political conviction rested on "the greatness of England and the infinity of England's mission, on the rights of ability to govern and on the natural kingship of the higher races." [5]) He hated popular government and democracy in general and his opinion about the miners of his collieries betrayed this aversion: "I detest them, pigheaded brutes! They will be on strike next month and I shall be defrauded of my lawful income till their lordships choose to go back." [6])

He was acquainted with Lord and Lady Maxwell. Lord Maxwell introduced a factory-act for East-London, according to which it was punishable for the labourer to work in his own house and it limited the number of workinghours. Mrs. Ward had studied the factory-problem seriously, for her son-in-law says that she "had taken much pains to learn every detail of the system of sweated homework prevalent in the East End of London at that time, wading through piles of Bluebooks, visiting the actual scene under the care of a Factory inspector." [7])

Sir George and Lady Maxwell differ in opinion about the necessity of State-interference on behalf of the labourers. (Mrs. Ward draws attention to the fact, that the State entirely left the improvement of social conditions to philanthropic societies

---

[1]) Mrs. Humphry Ward, *Sir George Tressady*, Smith and Elder's ed., p. 360.
[2]) ibid., p. 2.   [3]) ibid., p. 3.   [4]) ibid., p. 94.   [5]) ibid., p. 46.
[6]) ibid., p. 234.
[7]) G. M. Trevelyan, *The Life of Mrs. Humphry Ward*, Ch. VI, p. 115.

and private persons, among whom Toynbee, whose work became well-known all over the world, took up an important place). Lady Maxwell considered it the duty of the state but Sir George's opinion was : "So long as men are slaves by law, there is always a chance for freedom. Anyway 'we' stand for freedom — as an end, not a means. It is 'not' the business of the State to make people happy — not at all ! — at least that is our view — but it 'is' the business of the State to keep them free." [1]) Hoping that her friend might come to an other conclusion, she urged him to go and see some places where home-industry was at its worst. She asked him to visit her in her home in Mile End Road, (which her husband and herself inhabited during the week to be in contact with the labourers) that he should see what people are like "after having worked fourteen hours at a stretch in a room where you and I could not breathe." His opinion did not alter ; he still felt for his leader's motives, but it raised in him "a number of piercing questions, which George Tressady would never have raised.... if it had not been for a woman and a woman's charm." [2]) As for the Bill, he did not think much of its workings and he felt bound to his leader's cause with which were linked "his own personal honour and fidelity and his pledges to his constituents and his party." [3]) The long discussions in Parliament loosened his originally Calvinistic conviction. Lady Maxwell's anxiety about her husband's disappointment in case the bill should not be passed made him deliver a speech, which was "a political event of the first order."[4]) "He tore to pieces Fontenoy's elaborate attack, showed what practical men thought of the clause and with what careful reliance upon their opinion and their experience it had been framed, and finally.... announced his intentions of voting with the government." [5]) The law passed with a majority of twenty-six votes. In a quarrel with his wife afterwards he confessed why he had disappointed his leader : "I should never have taken

---

[1]) Mrs. Humphry Ward, *Sir George Tressady*, p. 109.
[2]) ibid., p. 284.   [3]) ibid., p. 283.   [4]) ibid., p. 406.   [5]) ibid., p. 407.

the part I did.... but that I had come to have a strong wish — to give Lady Maxwell her heart's desire." [1] Lady Maxwell told him that his speech would save many people, but he answered: "I never thought of them at all.... As for the thing itself.... I had simply come to think that what you wished was good. A force I no longer questioned drove me to help you to your end. That was the whole secret of last night." [2]

Lady Maxwell's influence on him proceeded from his own unhappy married life. She succeeded in bringing about a better understanding between the hero and his frivolous, selfish wife. They went to live at their estate in the North, where he lost his life in a colliery accident, when he put to practice the new democratic ideas in trying to save his miners. His death was heroic after all.

Mrs. Humphry Ward made a blunder in creating this hero. He is simply a background against which the charming personality of Lady Maxwell is outlined. That he had the courage to face a whole House of Lords, with an open avowal of his admiration for his opponent's ideas, is a deed of great moral force, which, according to Mr. J. Exner's researches,[3] must have been suggested by Lord Randolph Churchill, who on March 7th 1878 attacked the leader of his party and also voted with the opposition. It would have been more honourable if the hero had come to this conclusion after long thinking and after weighing in the balance the pros and cons of Lady Maxwell's arguments. Mrs. Humphry Ward only forces home upon the reader the influence of the heroine's personality on the hero, not considering that by doing so she made of this character a weak individual, a man without a back-bone, who suffered his political opinions to be influenced by the state of his matrimonial affairs. Men like Sir George Tressady ought not to take a seat in Parliament. The welfare of a country should be dependent only on the government of strong-willed persons of firm convictions and not on men

---

[1] ibid., p. 415.   [2] ibid., p. 423.
[3] J. Exner, *Mrs. Humphry Wards Tendenzromane*, Breslau Diss. 1912.

who, because of personal disappointment, suffer themselves to waver from their cause to please a woman with an attractive face. The hero makes the impression that "his mind was a chaos, without convictions, either intellectual or moral; that he had begun what he was not able to finish and that he was doomed to make a failure of his parliamentary career." [1]) Of this he himself was fully aware, when he was sitting in Parliament, listening to the speeches for and against Maxwell's bill.

Both the heroes, Lord Maxwell and Sir George Tressady, as opponent of the heroine, serve as mouth-pieces to proclaim the novelist's views of the leading social difficulties. One critic, Mr. Sidney Webb, wrote in an undated letter his approval of her labour in the words: "You have managed to give the arguments for and against factory-legislation and a fixed standard of life with admirable lucidity and picturesqueness — in a way that will make them comprehensible to the ordinary person without any technical knowledge."

In this way Mrs. Ward, who only came into contact with the poor, when she visited them, expressed through her heroes her great longing for the improvement of their lot.

Mrs. Humphry Ward was invited to deliver some lectures in America and availed herself of this opportunity to pay a visit to Canada also. Her experiences, and the impression this colony made upon her, she wrote down in a novel, the hero being "the personification of that vigorous, young colony, embodying in itself its efforts and its aspirations." [2]) The hero, George Anderson, was "a remarkably handsome, well-made fellow," [3]) "tall, fair, with a blond moustache and very blue eyes." [4]) He was a man of moral independence in his nature, of loathing for any habit that weakens and enslaves the will." [5]) He was very proud of Canada, as being a part of the great Empire but he said: "we have our own future...., we are loyal to a common ideal, a common

---
[1]) Mrs. Humphry Ward, *Sir George Tressady*, p. 280.
[2]) J. Stuart Walters, *Mrs. Humphry Ward, Her Work and Influence*, p. 170.
[3]) Mrs. Humphry Ward, *Canadian Born*, Smith and Elder's ed., p. 29.
[4]) ibid., p. 27.   [5]) ibid., p. 167.

mission in the world...., we stand together. We march together. But Canada will have her own history; and you must not try to make it for her." [1]) He said this to a lady, who was of opinion that England and Canada were one state. A fierce hatred of the Americans, who want to take possession of the country but do not want to become Canadians, filled him. This love of Canada inspired the heroine with admiration. He met her in a railway-accident, when she was making a tour through Canada with her brother. "She was impressed by the varied life that the man's personality produced on her. Her sympathies and imagination were all trembling towards the Canadian." [2]) She wrote to her mother: "he seems to embody the very life of this country, to be the prairie and the railway and the forest — their very spirit and avatar.... His life has been hard, yet the heart of him is all hope and courage, all delight too in the daily planning and wrestling, the contrivance and the cleverness, the rifling and outwitting of Nature." [3]) He became her brother's friend and kept him from drinking, because he knew from experience to what a man may come who is addicted to liquor. In his youth he had lost his mother and four sisters when his father in a fit of drunkenness had set their farm on fire. He and his brothers had worked till they had money enough to study; in this way he himself had become an engineer. Now he wanted to go into politics and was already a 'person' in the North West. His behaviour during the great strike, his influence on both master and hands, had drawn the attention of leading persons to him. He had just got a letter from the Dominion Prime Minister, in which he was offered "a mission of enquiry to England on some important matters connected with labour and emigration. The letter was remarkable, addressed to a man so young and on the threshold of a political career." [4])

Suddenly his father, of whom he had heard nothing since the fatal fire and whom he supposed was dead, appeared. He did all he could for the old drunkard who succeeded in

---

[1]) ibid., p. 180.   [2]) ibid., p. 41.   [3]) ibid., p. 117.   [4]) ibid., p. 179.

coming into contact with other ruffians. This gang brought a train to a stand-still, wanting to rob the travellers. In the ensuing struggle his father was shot. Anderson was so much ashamed of his father's behaviour, "though he knew himself sound, intellectually and morally," [1]) that he wanted to give up his political career and decline the minister's request. Letters from friends, the minister's firm refusal to accept his letter, and the heroine's pleadings induced him to change his mind. He wanted to have Elizabeth for his wife, but supposed she was unwilling to leave England and all her connections there, and he felt, in spite of his love, that he would not be able to give up Canada and live in England. Elizabeth, however, had no such scruples. They were married and settled in the Northwest of the colony, which she had learned to love through his enthusiasm.

Mrs. Ward shows in this character a type of man who will make colonization a success. He possesses courage, energy, sympathy and resourcefulness. He is the off-spring of the men who slowly but surely took the expansion of the motherland in hand. Still feeling the link that binds them to it, they, however, want to make of their new fatherland an independent self-governing country, whose future is destined to be as brilliant as has been the past of the mother-country. Men like George Anderson, "the indomitable colonial, have made our colonies the wonder and envy of the world." [2])

Firmin Roz's statement is quite to the point : "George Anderson est la personnification du pays neuf, de la race jeune, de ses efforts, de ses espoirs." [3]) In creating him the authoress "paid her debt to Canada by the delightful enthusiasm for the young country with all its boundless possibilities combined with a shrewd appreciation of its difficulties." [4])

It is not his personal life, his thoughts, his love for his relations and his bride, which occupied the author's thoughts in

---
[1]) ibid., p. 143.
[2]) J. Stuart Walters, *Mrs. Humphry Ward, Her Work and Influence*, p. 194.
[3]) *Revue des Deux Mondes*, 15 Mars, 1910.
[4]) G. M. Trevelyan, *The Life of Mrs. Humphry Ward*, p. 222.

describing this hero, but his energy, his ambition, his enthusiasm for the future of his country, all which do not concern the emotional part of his character.

André Chevalley observes : "Grâce à Mrs. Humphry Ward nous avons parcouru quelques-unes des régions les plus interessantes de la pensée de l'action et de l'existence dans les zones les plus cultivées de l'Angleterre." [1]) She has done this by means of her heroes. They are paintings of characters in modern environments. She has placed them in circumstances, issuing from spiritual troubles. Though not in actual contact with the poor, she has shown her longing to improve their condition through her political heroes, and gave an insight into the personality of the men who have made 'greater England'.

Mrs. Ward followed the same method as her predecessors. She found her heroes among the people with whom she conversed. Her principal male characters display their creator's psychological insight as well as her many-sided intellectual development, though in quite a different way from George Eliot. The latter showed a one-sided development of her gifted mind. She created her later heroes simply for the purpose of moral instruction. She was not interested in religious problems, nor did she meddle with politics. In this respect she is very different from Mrs. Ward, whose heroes were leading politicians and clergyman who took an active part in the improvement of existing wrongs. They were naturally depicted, though somewhat one-sided, as full justice was not done to the love-affair which also has its share in a man's life. These heroes may be termed 'heroes of culture'.

In these heroes the present writer found for the first time a reflection of the novelist's ripened mind and matured convictions with respect to her political and religious views. Neither Robert Elsmere, nor Aldous Raeburn or Helbeck of Bannisdale are convincing proofs of strong personalities. The one gives up

---

[1]) A. Chevalley, *Le Roman Anglais de notre Temps*, p. 52.

the Church to which he had plighted his word without great inward struggle, because he had embraced its creed on very loose grounds. The political views of Raeburn work slowly and want stirring up. It is true, he sees the desirability of a more democratic government, but his deep-rooted dislike to change makes him adhere to the old conservatism. The third constantly wavers between his earthly and his spiritual love and by this causes the death of his newly regained bride. Mrs. Ward pictured by the side of each of these three a self-willed, energetic, enthusiastic young woman, who does not for a moment think of giving up her firmly-rooted opinions and ideas, and who, through her conduct, brings the hero's weakness into prominence. The heroes of this novelist's later years are strong-willed, vigorous, resolute persons. Richard Meynell does not think of leaving the Church; in his opinion the Church had to admit the dissenters. George Anderson would have sacrificed his own hopes of future domestic happiness to be able to serve the colony to which he had pledged his life. Their views also roused enthusiasm in their heroines, who, though not the dependent, self-sacrificing girls of a former century, are quite willing to entrust their future to these forceful characters.

It is not possible to detect Mrs. Ward's wish to proclaim a special doctrine or to attract attention to a certain characteristic. In the heroes of all the preceding novelists the embodiment is seen of a central idea, which occupies the novelist's mind. At first it is love, then human sympathy, which is a form of love, and at last the hero has become the mouthpiece of some doctrine. This well-known 'family-likeness' cannot be traced in Mrs. Ward's heroes. The qualities to which she wished to attract attention in her heroes are according to Mr. Stuart Walters, "character, tenacity of purpose, a strong sense of duty and a keen appreciation of the importance of moral dignity." [1] She wanted to deal with leading subjects and she did full justice to them.

---

[1] J. Stuart Walters, *Mrs. Humphry Ward, Her Work and Influence*, p. 170.

Mr. Firmin Roz states in his criticism that "Madame Humphry Ward a su aborder les principales questions de l'heure présente, questions religieuses, morales, sociales, politiques même. Elle les a traitées dans l'esprit de son temps et de son pays." [1]) It is the vitality of her genius, the perfection of her craftmanship, which enabled Mrs. Ward to hold a first place among contemporary novelists.

Mrs. Humphry Ward is the first female writer and inspirer of a group of novelists who have given their attention and thoughts to current questions. In the beginning they were religious or political problems that came up for discussion, but in course of time, it was especially the rights of woman, her enfranchisement and suffrage, the revision of matrimonial legislation and equality of man and woman, which suggested themselves as subjects for the novels; the hero represented the advanced views of the authors. In view of the endless train of female writers, who entered the field of English letters after Mrs. Ward, the present writer thought it best to finish her discussion with the heroes of this woman, who gave the impetus.

---

[1]) *Revue des Deux Mondes*, 15 Mars, 1910.

CHAPTER XV.

SUMMARY.

New Types.

From the heroes described it is evident that many new heroes are due to the inventive female mind. Aphra Behn launched a hero, outside the general style, yet attractive and interesting. She called into being a host of imitators, male as well as female. Her life and adventures can be put on the same line with those of men; it is no wonder, that she created a hero, who may be ranked among the best creations of the other sex.

Fanny Burney, though following in the wake of Richardson, gave for the first time through her hero's life a faithful presentation of the manners of ordinary, actual living people.

Mrs. Inchbald strayed from the then current type by taking a former Roman-Catholic priest for her principal character, who did not at all cut a bad figure by the side of the clergyman already created. "Es ist interessant zu sehen, dasz der katholische Geistliche nicht als Vicar of Wakefield geschaut wird, sondern einem selbständigen Typus beginnt," [1] Dibelius states.

Maria Edgeworth, applying the same method as Miss Burney did by taking her hero from among the people by whom she was surrounded, was the first to describe national characteristics through her heroes. By this she influenced Sir Walter Scott and many others.

Half a century afterwards Charlotte Brontë appeared with a hero, who was quite an innovation. Her sister Emily surprised

---

[1] W. Dibelius, *Englische Romankunst*, Band II, Ch. 9, p. 20.

the reading public with the picture of a villain, such as was unknown in the history of the novel.

George Eliot created in Tito Melema a character that is "une des plus originales et peut-être la plus neuve qu'il y ait dans la littérature entière de ce siècle. Celui-la est absolument sans précédents, je [Mons. E. Montégut] ne lui découvre aucune resemblance ni prochaine, ni lointaine, avec aucun autre personage du monde de la fiction." [1]) C'est une maîtresse main qui a tracé ce portrait, mais y fallait que cette main fût celle d'une femme, car quelle main masculine aurait été d'un tact assez délicat et d'une adresse assez patiente pour cette tâche compliquée et subtile ? [2])

Lord Crewe, one of the critics of Mrs. Humphry Ward's novels, observed that Helbeck of Bannisdale was "as fresh a creation as Ravenswood or Rochester" and that it was "a luxury to hang a new portrait on one's walls in this age of old figures in patched garments." [3])

The Hero. (Imitation and Influence of Male Authors.)

In the chapters on the first woman-novelists the resemblance of the heroes to Richardson's Sir Charles Grandison has been pointed out more than once and in the subsequent investigations the present writer has repeatedly spoken of imitation of this prototype or of his influence. It is true, these heroes unmistakably bear the image of Sir Charles Grandison, if this hero is 'the perfect gentleman' and not the insufferable, conceited egotist. She wishes, however, also to point out, that though the influence of this prototype is certainly often traceable, the fact must not be lost sight of that the influence of each novelist's surroundings is also a factor not to be neglected. Due attention must be paid

---
[1]) E. Montégut, *Ecrivains Modernes de l'Angleterre*, George Eliot, Portrait général, p. 141.
[2]) ibid., p. 137.
[3]) G. M. Trevelyan, *The Life of Mrs. Humphry Ward*, Ch. VIII, p. 143.

to the fact that Frances Burney wrote from observation only, that Mrs. Inchbald's friends recognized in Dorriforth her admirer Kemble, that Jane Austen and Maria Edgeworth pictured their characters in general and consequently their heroes also with amazing naturalness. The present writer has come to the conviction that the gentlemen of the times of these authoresses must also have had characteristics and qualities similar, if inferior, to Grandison's, and must have behaved in the domestic circle in a manner recalling that same paragon.

A man like this hero, the perfection of the courteous knight of the old romances, appealed most to women with their narrow social experience. He was for them a living being and spoke to their imaginations. It is certain that Richardson knew the feminine mind so well, that he was able to create a hero, who answered this ideal to perfection. One of Miss Edgeworth's heroines gave a description of the hero of her heart: "I had early in my secret soul, as perhaps you have at this instant in yours, a pattern of perfection — something chivalrous, noble, something that is no longer to be seen now-a-days — the more delightful to imagine, the moral sublime and beautiful; more than human, yet with the extreme of human tenderness. Mine was to be a demigod, whom I could worship, a husband to whom I could always look up, with whom I could always sympathize, and to whom I could devote myself with all a woman's self-devotion." [1]) This quotation proves that the ideal of the feminine mind at that time bore a striking resemblance to Richardson's hero, i. e. an embodiment of peculiar nobility and distinctive beauty. Most probably the novelists took for their hero the man who was specially endowed with such characteristics as they saw in the ideal of their own hearts.

Women during that period were often deficient in learning. All of them, Mrs. Inchbald excepted, lived rather secluded lives, and had little intercourse with men, except in society. Their experiences, as the Vicar of Wakefield said of his own, were

---

[1]) Maria Edgeworth, *Helen*, p. 68.

limited to the fireside. With reference to representing a character Henry Fielding observes: "The picture must be after nature herself. A true knowledge of the world is gained only by conversation, and the manners of every rank must be seen in order to be known." [1]) Hence the faithful pictures of heroes moving in society. However, such heroes grow insipid. By and by, though the original pattern of perfection was retained, certain flaws came to be admitted in the portrayal of the hero. Such heroes are rather more life-like. The more Richardson's "beau ideal of manly virtue" [2]) fades, the more natural the domestic hero grows till he reaches his full development in Jane Austen's works.

When the standard types of the preceding century had been effaced from the general mind and women began to move about in the world, they portrayed also heroes outside the family circle. Though Richardson's influence is not spoken of in the descriptions of the heroes of the later novelists, it is, of course, quite possible to discover in those characters, nay in any hero, a Grandison. Dibelius says that "jede Fortentwicklung der menschlichen Vollkommenheit muss ja notwendig dazu führen, Schwächen zu entdecken; auf diese Weise nähert sich der Grandisontype mehr und mehr dem des Tom Jones." [3]) In the first heroes these characteristics are more conspicuous as their behaviour in society is chiefly treated. When the principal figures are taken from everyday people, and are seen in their daily occupations, other qualities demand our attention.

Before Charlotte Brontë took to 'portrait painting' she and her sister Emily enriched English literature with novels whose heroes entitle them to a separate place in the line of lady-novelists. Both stand entirely apart from their predecessors in creating heroes chiefly based on fantasy. They form a landmark in our survey of heroes, for the characters they depict, surpass by their wickedness any hero produced up till then in the novel

---

[1]) H. Fielding, *Tom Jones*, Bk. XIV, Ch. I.
[2]) W. Raleigh, *The English Novel*, Ch. VI, p. 154.
[3]) W. Dibelius, *Englische Romankunst*, Band II, p. 361.

by male writers of fiction. Hugh Walter is right in his conclusion that "a fervid imagination and a fast capacity of wrath, operating upon the combined lives of the Brontës, produced *Jane Eyre* and *Wuthering Heights*." [1]) As for the heroes of her other novels Charlotte Brontë introduced quite a new genre. She was the first to produce carefully drawn portraits of beings who pass through a series of events of which she has been a close witness. In her works there is a beginning of realism, but still mingled with the old romanticism.

Subsequently in the novels of her female contemporaries, realism fully set in. They continued her method of giving the results of personal experience, but began to focus full light on their heroes' actions. Mrs. Gaskell's psychology does not go very deep and is not the result of intellectual study, but of sympathy with her fellow-creatures. The difficulties and troubles in which her heroes are involved are rather sufferings produced by circumstances than agonies of heart and mind. However, she marks the birth of the emotional element in the character of the hero who is henceforth treated as an intricate complex of vices and virtues, i. e. as a real human being.

The world judges from appearances and pity is only roused, when it is allowed a peep behind the scenes. Mrs. Gaskell who wanted to call forth sympathy through the description of her heroes' lives, readily achieved her object by giving her readers an insight into the lives both of manufacturers and factory-hands. George Eliot continued to reveal in her first period, besides psychological insight, also Mrs. Gaskell's realism. In her early works her instinctive sympathy enabled her to draw heroes so real and natural, that they showed her literary gifts to the full. She and her contemporaries drew from real life, from observation, and from experience.

Professor Saintsbury is no doubt right in asserting that "every author is more or less dependent on personal experience ; it is not only legitimate, but an almost invariable part of the novelist's

---

[1]) Hugh Walter, *The Literature of the Victorian Era*, p. 170.

resources." [1]) Unless an author has an endless variety of examples at his disposal, his stock of characters gets exhausted. It is then "rather a mine than a fertile field, which can be cropped year after year." [2]) The Brontës and Mrs. Gaskell died before they became aware that their stock of examples had given out, but George Eliot's works distinctly betray exhaustion. She then resorts to a new kind of heroes who are nothing but abstractions. Starting from an idea or principle, the novelist invested this conception with a semblance of reality. The lives of Mrs. Gaskell's heroes also serve as a moral, interpreting the novelist's opinion on the existing discords, though she never meddled with any political or religious question. George Eliot followed this method in her second period, and consequently became "a very curious instance of the danger of self-education." [3]) Creations may approximate to realities ; yet an author is apt to overdo a character in his enthusiasm to make his idea understood. This is the case with George Eliot. Her increasing intellectual development, her philosophical studies, her little contact with the world and consequent scanty experience, all these influences combined resulted in creating heroes like Tito Melema and Daniel Deronda. Mr. Harold Williams explains very clearly what was wanting in such figures: "nothing in nature or in human nature is plainly expository of any ethical or religious idea, save that brought to it by the spectator. And great art has no neat and unmistakable doctrines of life and conduct. Experience is action and reaction between man and his environment." [4])

George Eliot stands apart from her contemporaries, and also from Mrs. Humphry Ward, another woman of great intellect and an equally ardent student. "Mrs. Humphry Ward partit du roman à thèse pour aboutir au roman politique et mondain," [5]) is André Chevalley's verdict. This latter novelist sought to influence the great religious, political and social movements, and

[1]) G. Saintsbury, *A Short History of English Literature*, p. 749.
[2]) H. Walter, *The Literature of the Victorian Era*, p. 736.
[3]) Edmund Gosse, *Modern English Literature*, p. 372.
[4]) H. Williams, *Modern English Writers*, p. 423.
[5]) A. Chevalley, *Le Roman anglais de notre Temps*, p. 51.

saw in the hero of the novel a convenient personage to acquaint the world with her opinions on the possible solutions of the problems. As her heroes proclaim ideas of actual interest, and are modelled on persons with whom she was in contact, her characters bear the unmistakable stamp of truth. Though lacking spontaneity, they are not mere lay-figures. Her heroes, although they have been created with a purpose, fulfill Hudson's requirements, stated as follows: "the first thing we require of any novelist in his handling of character is that, whether he keeps close to common experience or boldly experiments with the fantastic and the abnormal, his men and women shall move through his pages like living beings." [1]

Just as the first authoress were considered to have 'moulded' their heroes after an existing example, Mrs. Gaskell, and Charlotte Brontë have been classed among those who did not produce original work. It is said that their heroes are manifestly modelled on those of Dickens. With regard to this it may be observed, (vide Professor Minto's article on *Mary Barton*) that the same thought may arise and ripen in the minds of more than one author. Their treating the same subject does not imply imitation. In the middle of the nineteenth century women were not inclined to pronounce their opinions so openly, and needed some cause that roused them to do so. It is quite possible, though, that these ladies borrowed their ideas from the male authors. At any rate they solved the problems quite satisfactorily in their own ways.

Mrs. Gaskell in the manufacturer Thornton, George Eliot in her workmen-heroes, as well Adam Bede as Felix Holt, reveal themselves as upholders of Carlyle's theories on the nobility of work. The admiration which was generally felt for Carlyle these authoresses expressed through their heroes.

Mrs. Humphry Ward treated with great success the themes tackled by her male contemporaries, but the suggestion of

---

[1] W. H. Hudson, *An Introduction to the Study of Literature*, p. 190.

influence or imitation is out of place in her case, though she may have profited by the novels of others.

The only case in which imitation is conspicuous is in George Eliot's Daniel Deronda and this hero was generally considered a failure.

Love-aspect.

When the present writer began this study, she expected to find in every hero a reflection of the author's ideal developed more and more clearly in the successive novels of each authoress. In this expectation she has been disappointed, however. The heroes of the three last authoresses, who were all married women, fall short in projecting the novelist's own ideal hero. Though they all three took their heroes from their immediate surroundings, not one of them either used her husband as a model for her principal male character or based her own idealised conception on him. In a superficial way the earlier women-novelists, who, with the exception of Mrs. Inchbald, were all unmarried, revealed their ideal of the other sex through their heroes. Only once is the ideal of the heart or at least the nearest approximation to it really met with: Charlotte Brontë created such a hero, thanks to the straightforward manner in which she expressed without reticence the longing that was in her heart.

Aphra Behn was the first and only female-author who gave a successful blend of the hero's love-affairs and the questions she wanted to satirize. She stands quite alone in this respect. It is remarkable that the other novelists treated either the one or the other. The pioneers pictured only the hero's relation towards the object of his love. In their works the love-story takes up the principal place and everything turns on this. For the description of love-moods they could use their fantasy, imagination, intuition and personal experience. This forms a noticeable difference with the later authoresses, in whose novels other aspects of the hero's life are considered.

The moral aspects in George Eliot's, and the social and religious questions in Mrs. Humphry Ward's works, take up such an important part in the lives of their heroes, that their attitudes towards the heroine have become of secondary importance. The love-interest is treated superficially and only with relation to the humanitarian cause espoused by the hero, or, it may be, to give additional point to the moral.

The hero's character and his feelings towards the object of his love may be gathered from his conversations with the other personages, i. e. by dramatic characterisation. This helps to make the reader's interest in the hero increase who appears the more human. The passages quoted show that this method was much in favour among the first novelists. Hudson aptly remarks that "it is always better that a character should be made to reveal itself than that it should be dissected from the outside." [1] The hero of 'pure creation' on the other hand is explained and commented on by the author. George Eliot often sets forth her characters in lengthy explanations. Daniel Deronda is a striking example of this method. Mrs. Ward often causes her heroes to express her views in the course of their conversation or in speeches. Richard Meynell surpasses all the other heroes in this respect. Hudson urgently warns against applying this method too much, for "where dissection is perpetually substituted for self-revelation, it is often because the novelist is deficient in true dramatic sense and power." [2] Maria Edgeworth, Jane Austen and Mrs. Gaskell use a combination of the two methods by making the heroes speak for themselves and by commenting occasionally upon their actions.

Outward appearance.

The hero's outward appearance does not take up much room in the novels of the early authoresses. Only Aphra Behn gives a

---

[1] W. H. Hudson, *An Introduction to the Study of English Literature*, p. 194.
[2] ibid., p. 194.

very long description, perhaps because she introduced a hero unknown up till then in literary history, and not often seen at that time. Mrs. Inchbald also in one place pictured her hero's appearance. Neither Clara Reeve, Mrs. Radcliffe nor Miss Edgeworth on the other hand, waste one word on their heroes' faces or bearings. Charlotte Brontë describes the persons of her heroes rather minutely, a method continued by George Eliot and Mrs. Ward, the latter providing attractive bodily mansions for her conceptions to dwell in.

Profession.

It cannot be said that the woman-writers favour any special profession. The earlier ladies take their heroes from among the better classes, because they chiefly associated with the gentry and people of standing. Their occupations, however, have nothing to do with the story and consequently no attention is paid to them. The 'portraits' represent everyday people. The 'heroes of creation' belong to the better classes, as it is naturally from the intellectual world that intellectual leaders are recruited. Of all professions that of a clergyman has found most favour; among the heroes we find no physician, lawyer, actor or military officer. It is true, Mrs. Radcliffe's Valancourt is an officer, but this fact is only mentioned by the way.

The Age.

The hero's age has little to do with the age of the authoress at the time she wrote her novel, but it is quite logical that other qualities and characteristics should be looked for and expected in a hero by a woman when she is young than at a maturer age. The ideal, or an approximation to it, of a woman between twenty and twenty-five is quite another person with other characteristics than the partner for life, whom she hopes to find, when she is past thirty-five. She makes other demands with regard to physical and mental qualities, but she is also on the look-out for that maturity of character which comes only with years. So it is quite natural that the hero of Frances Burney, Jane Austen and Mrs. Radcliff is a very young man. It might be expected that the hero of the authoresses who started novel-writing at the age of about forty would be a man a little above this age. However, he is not, and this furnishes a proof that the hero is not a reflection of the novelist's own hero.

Religion.

Religion exerts a far greater influence than does age. Aphra Behn pronounced through Oronooko her dislike for the degraded state to which religion had fallen at the end of the seventeenth century. Mrs. Inchbald described how her Catholic hero renounced his ecclesiastical profession in order to be able to marry and to secure an heir to his property. Charlotte Brontë, unconventional as ever, makes her best hero persuade the heroine to be converted to Catholicism. Though not a Roman-Catholic herself, she represents him as a staunch Roman-Catholic. Adam Bede is the personification of George Eliot's sound, religiously formed ideal of humanity. In Daniel Deronda this novelist created a champion for the Jews and their cause; whilst she had entered upon her literary career by enlisting her readers' sympathy for the lives of three insignificant clergymen. To Mrs. Humphry Ward honour is due for creating a Roman-Catholic hero whose mental struggles concerning his love for the heroine form the subject. She pictured in a striking manner the hero's faith in and love for the church to which he has devoted himself, and the earthly love for the girl that comes across his path. Robert Elsmere and Richard Meynell are two heroes who had to proclaim Mrs. Ward's views regarding the existing faith in the Anglican Church at the time she wrote the novels.

Interest in politics.

It is a remarkable fact that, though the early lady-novelists lived in a period which may be called one of the most interesting in the history of Europe, not one made her hero even hint at the turbulent times or at the hardships, privations, and anxieties which this period brought along with it. Aphra Behn again makes an exception; she attacked abuses in government through her hero's mouth in veiled terms, as her male colleagues used to do. It cannot possibly be accepted that women did not know anything of what was going on in Europe and in their own country, but it may be taken for granted that it was not considered proper for a lady to speak of those affairs. Of the later authoresses who wrote at a time when nobody minded public opinion, only Mrs. Gaskell makes her heroes take an active part in the industrial troubles of her time. Charlotte Brontë's hero, Robert Moore, is also involved in troubles resulting from his ownership of a factory and the introduction of new machinery into it. These are the troubles of the beginning of the century, which she studied from books and old newspapers but not those of her own period. Charlotte Brontë as well as George Eliot were well-acquainted with conditions abroad and at home, but neither of the two was interested in political questions. Mrs. Humphry Ward's active mind on the contrary was always occupied with social problems and she uses her heroes only and exclusively as mouth-pieces of her opinions.

The Heroines.

The girls on whom the heroes have fixed their eyes and hearts are invariably non-intellectual women. This simply confirms the fact that intellectual development had not reached its present stage, and that scientific study did not take up such a place in woman's life as it does at present. Women did not think of shifting for themselves by taking up a situation, which made them financially independent and which forced them to compete with male colleagues. The heroines of Mrs. Ward's novels already mark a difference, for all the heroes, except Sir George Tressady, fall in love with strong-willed ladies, who hold their own opinions on the questions of the day and are not so easily persuaded to give up their unmarried state. Mr. Stuart Walters draws special attention to two of these heroes when he says that "she created in Aldous Raeburn and Helbeck of Bannisdale the only men of strong individuality that became husbands of strong women." [1])

The idea of marriage was that both husband and wife should "constitute the happiness of each other ; the same taste, the same noble and benevolent sentiments animating each." [2]) Mutual respect and confidence were, however, also considered foundations of married life at the end of the eighteenth century. Hence the spirit of the time does not allow a hero to have anything to do with a woman whose life does not bear the stamp of unsullied reputation. Mrs. Inchbald's hero refuses any intercourse with his wife after her misconduct during his absence on business and involves his little daughter in his hatred. Frances Burney's and Maria Edgeworth's heroes go further ; they try to give up any thought of the girls they have chosen and sacrifice them to their Puritanical notions, when they hear that unions with them would prove to be blots on their own family-names. In her last novel, however, Miss Edgeworth takes up a more advanced point of view, when the hero remains the loyal, devoted lover in spite of what is said of his fiancée. Jane Austen goes still further : Darcy knew that Elizabeth was not of his standing, yet he wants her for his wife in spite of this. But he was conscious of his condescension in proposing to Elizabeth and told her as much.

The Heroine's views of the Hero.

Striking examples of the heroine's influence on the hero's character are made in Jane Austen's Darcy and Mrs. Gaskell's

---
[1]) J. Stuart Walters, *Mrs. Humphry Ward*, p. 80.
[2]) Mrs. A. Radcliffe, *The Mysteries of Udolpho*, Vol. I, Ch. XIII, p. 70.

Thorton, who both change their behaviour, which hurts the heroine's feelings, when they learn to see that they are wrong. Caroline Helstone in Charlotte Brontë's *Shirley* also tries to bring about a change, though not in a very resolute way. Helbeck of Bannisdale on the other hand proves that the heroine has no influence whatever.

A noticeable difference from the respect with which the other heroes treat their heroines is given in those of the sisters Brontë. Laura Marholm has said very appropriately with regard to these heroes: "Was das Weib beim Manne sucht — das ist Schutz.... Das ist der Grund weshalb noch heute dem Weibe der starke Mann über den schönen Mann geht und Muskeln über geistige Reize." [1] In respect to the other heroines the rest of her statement applies better : "Der Mann, der Mann ist kraft seiner geistigen und seelischen Eigenschaften, und nicht nur kraft seiner Muskeln, wird dem verfeinerten und beseelten Weib weit über den Athleten gehen, weil er ihr eine vollkommnere Form des Schutzes gewähren kann, als jener." [2]

---

[1] L. Marholm, *Zur Psychologie der Frau,* Ch. VIII, p. 280.
[2] ibid.

CONCLUSION.

In the preceding chapters the present writer has tried to point out that the history of the heroes conceived and portrayed by feminine writers of fiction, is at the same time the history of the natural development of the feminine mind and of the position women take up in society. When the women of the late eighteenth and early nineteenth centuries had broken the bonds of their domestic confinement, and forced their way into the ranks of authors, they had also made themselves indispensable.

The novelists that have been discussed, whether they wrote love-stories or took to dissecting character, described their heroes as they saw men and gave their solutions of leading questions in their own ways. Now that public opinion does not keep women from occupying and accepting all sorts of situations which allow them to move in every circle on the same footing as men, and all branches of study are open to them, their insight into persons and problems will develop all the better. This freedom will give women entirely different conceptions of various subjects, conceptions which must come nearer to those of men.

They will portray their heroes with much more freedom, and this may lead to a hero, who is the novelist's ideal as well as the spokesman of her views.

Greater intellectual development and freer association with the other sex may help intuition in creating life-like characters. Nevertheless, unless the authoress is a woman of extraordinary insight the writer of this thesis considers it impossible for her to picture the mental characteristics of a man, and to explain and understand his deeds and their motives as accurately and in such detail as she could in the case of a member of her own sex. Being a woman herself and holding this opinion, she sides with Sir Leslie Stephen, who rightly asserts that "men drawn by women, even by the ablest, are never quite of the masculine gender." [1]

---

[1] Leslie Stephen, *George Eliot,* Ch. V, p. 74.

BIBLIOGRAPHY.

Austen, Jane. *Pride and Prejudice*, The World's Classics.
Austen, Jane. *Sense and Sensibility*, Tauchnitz ed.
Austen, Jane. *Mansfield Park*, Everyman's Library.
Austen, Jane. *Emma*, The World's Classics.
Bald, M. A. *Woman Writers of the XIXth Century*, Cambridge, 1923.
Beers, H. A. *A History of English Romanticism in the Eighteenth Century*, New-York, 1899.
Beers, H. A. *A History of English Romanticism in the Nineteenth Century*, New-York, 1899.
Behn, A. *Oroonoko or the Royal Slave*, In the edition entitled ; All the Histories and Novels written by the late Ingenius Mrs. Behn, London, 1718.
Birrell, A. *Life of Charlotte Brontë*, Great Writers Series, 1887.
The Bookman, Nov., 1919.
Bray, Ch. *Phases of Opinion and Experience during a long Life*.
Brontë, Ch. *The Professor*, Tauchnitz. ed.
Brontë, Ch. *Jane Eyre*, Collins' ed.
Brontë, Ch. *Shirley*, The Caxton novels.
Brontë, Ch. *Villette*, The World's Classics.
Brontë, E. *Wuthering Heights*, The World's Classics.
Brunetière, F. *Le Roman Naturaliste*, Paris 1883.
Burney, F. *Evelina*, Everyman's library.
Burney, F. *Cecilia*, George Bell and Sons, 1904.
Busken Huet, Ch. *Litterarische Fantasiën en Kritieken*. Deel VIII en XXI.

The Cambridge History.
Carlyle, Th. *Heroes and Heroworship,* Collins' Classics.
Carlyle, Th. *Past and Present,* Collins' Classics.
Carlyle, Th. *Miscellaneous Essays,* 4 Vol.
Carlyle, Th. *Sartor Resartus,* Collins' Classics.
Cazamian, L. *Le Roman Social en Angleterre,* Paris, 1904.
Cazamian, M. L. *Le Roman et les Idées en Angleterre,* Strasbourg Diss. 1923.
Chambers's Cyclopaedia of English Literature, London 1906—14.
Chevalley, A. *Le Roman anglais de notre Temps,* London, 1921.
Cooke, G. Willis. *George Eliot,* A critical Study of her Life, Writings and Philosophy, London, 1883.
Cornish, F. Warre. *Jane Austen,* London, 1913.
Courtney, W. L. *The Feminine Note in Fiction,* London, 1904.
Cross, J. W. *George Eliot's Life,* as related in her Letters and Journals, London, 1885.
Cross, W. L. *The Development of the English Novel,* New-York, 1916.
Dibelius, W. *Englische Romankunst,* Berlin, 1910.
Dickens, Ch. *Hard Times.*
Dictionary of National Biography.
Disraeli, B. *Tancred.*
Deutsche Rundschau, 1877.
Drew, E. A. *The Modern Novel,* London, 1926.
Dullemen, Dr. J. J. *Mrs. Gaskell,* Novelist and Biographer, Amsterdam Diss., 1924.
Edgeworth, M. *The Absentee,* Everyman's library.
Edgeworth, M. *Helen,* Baudrey's European Library, Paris 1834.
Edinburgh Review, Dec., 1849.
Eliot, George. *Scenes of Clerical Life,* Collins' Classics.
Eliot, George. *Adam Bede,* Nelson ed.
Eliot, George. *Romola,* Seaside Library, New-York.
Eliot, George. *Felix Holt,* Everyman's library.
Eliot, George. *Daniel Deronda,* Tauchnitz ed.

Elton, Oliver. *A Survey of English Literature, 1780—1830*, London, 1912.

Exner, Jozef. *Mrs. Humphry Wards Tendenzromane*, Breslau Dissert., 1912.

Falconer, J. A. *The Professor and Villette*, in *English Studies*, Vol. IX April 1927.

Fielding, H. *Tom Jones.*

Fortnightly Review, Vol. XXIV, 1878.

Gaskell, Mrs. E. C. *The Life of Charlotte Brontë*, Everyman's Library.

Gaskell, Mrs. E. C. *Mary Barton*, Everyman's library.

Gaskell, Mrs. E. C. *North and South*, Everyman's library.

Gaskell, Mrs. E. C. *Sylvia's Lovers*, Everyman's library.

Gosse, E. *A History of Eighteenth Century Literature*, London, 1889.

Gosse, E. *Modern English Literature*, New and Revised ed., London, 1905.

Green, J. R. *A Short History of the English People*, London, 1889.

Gwynn, Stephen. *Mrs. Humphry Ward*, London, 1917.

Inchbald, E. *A Simple Story*, Baudrey's European Library, Paris, 1850.

Haldane, E. S. *George Eliot and her Times*, London, 1927.

Hazlitt, W. *Lectures on the English Comic Writers*, London, 1902.

Hazlitt, W. *Sketches and Essays*, The World's Classics, 1903.

Heymans, G. *Die Psychologie der Frauen*, Heidelberg, 1910.

Hill, Constance. *Maria Edgeworth and her Circle in the Days of Buonaparte and Bourbon*, London, 1910.

Hudson, W. H. *An Introduction to the Study of Literature*, second enlarged ed., London, 1922.

Key, Ellen. *De misbruikte krachten der Vrouw*, Vertaling uit het Deensch van Ph. Wijsman, Amsterdam, 1898.

Kennedy, J. M. *English Literature, 1880—1905*, London, 1912.

Killen, Alice M. *Le Roman Terrifiant*, Paris, 1924.

Kluge, Dr. Med. *Männliches und Weibliches Denken*, Halle a. S., 1902.
Lanier, Sidney. *The English Novel*, New York, 1897.
Lawless, Emily. *Maria Edgeworth*, English Men of Letters, London, 1904.
Legouis and Cazamian. *A History of English Literature*, London, 1927.
Lichtenberger, A. *La Sòcialisme Utopique*, Paris, 1898.
Littlewood, S. R. *Elizabeth Inchbald and her Circle*, London, 1921.
Macauley, T. B. *History of England*, Vol. I, Everyman's Lib.
Macauley, T. B. *Critical and Historical Essays*, London, 1869.
Mac Intyre, Ch. F. *Ann Radcliffe in Relation to her Time*, Yale Dissert., New-Haven, 1920.
Malden, Mrs. Ch. *Jane Austen*, Eminent Women Series, London, 1889.
Marholm, L. *Zur Psychologie der Frau*, Berlin, 1897—1903.
Montégut, E. *Ecrivains Modernes de l'Angleterre*, Paris, 1885.
Monthly Review, Sept.-Dec., 1794.
Morgan, Ch. E. *The Rise of the Novel of Manners*, A Study of English Prose Fiction between 1600 and 1740, New York, 1911.
Polak, M. *Wuthering Heights*, in *Neophilologus*, 14e jaargang 1929.
Prinsen J. Lzn., Dr. J. *De Roman in de 18e Eeuw in West-Europa*, Groningen, 1925.
Quaterly Review, Dec., 1848.
Radcliffe, A. *The Mysteries of Udolpho*, Chiswick, 1923.
Raleigh, Sir Walter. *The English Novel*, London, 1922.
Reeve, Clara. *The Old English Baron*, London, 1826.
Revue des Deux Mondes.
Revue Germanique, Vol. V, 1919.
Revue Politique et Littéraire, 1873 en 1880.
Richardson, S. *Sir Charles Grandison*.
Rousseau, J. J. *Emile*, Tome I, Paris, 1808.

Saintsbury, G. *The English Novel*, London, 1927.
Saintsbury, G. *Three Mid-Century Novelists* in *The Collected Essays and Papers*, London 1923.
Saintsbury, G. *A Short History of English Literature*, London, 1917.
Scarborough, D. *The Supernatural in Modern English Fiction*, New York, 1917.
Scott, Sir Walter. *Lives of the Novelists*, The World's Classics.
Siegel, P. *Aphra Behn's Gedichte und Prosawerke* in *Anglia*, Vol. XXV, 1902.
Shorter, Cl. K. *Charlotte Brontë and her Circle*, London, 1896.
Shorter, Cl. K. *Charlotte Brontë and her Sisters*, London, 1905.
Smith, Goldwin. *Life of Jane Austen*, London, 1890.
Stephen, Leslie. *Hours in a Library*, London, 1877.
Stephen, Leslie. *History of English Thought in the 18th cent.*, London, 1876.
Stephen, Leslie. *George Eliot*, English Men of Letters, London, 1902.
Stephen, Leslie. *English Literature and Society in the 18th cent.*, 1903.
Summers, Montague. *The Works of Aphra Behn*, London, 1915.
Swinburne, A. Ch. *A Note on Charlotte Brontë*, London, 1877.
Trevelyan, Mrs. G. M. *The Life of Mrs. Humphry Ward*, London, 1923.
Villard, Léonie. *Jane Austen, Sa vie et son oeuvre*, Paris Diss., 1914.
Vooys, Dr. S. de. *The Psychological Element in the English Sociological Novel*, Amsterdam Diss., 1927.
Walker, Hugh. *The Literature of the Victorian Era*, Cambridge, 1910.
Walters, J. Stuart. *Mrs. Humphry Ward, Her Work and Influence*, London, 1912.
Ward, Mrs. Humphry. *Robert Elsmere*, Nelson, ed.
Ward, Mrs. Humphry. *Marcella*, Macmillon's Novelists' Library.
Ward, Mrs. Humphry. *Helbeck of Bannisdale*, Smith & Elder.

Ward, Mrs. Humphry. *Sir George Tressady*, Smith & Elder.
Ward, Mrs. Humphry. *The Case of Richard Meynell*, Smith & Elder.
Ward, Mrs. Humphry. *Canadian Born*, Smith & Elder.
Waugh, Arthur. *Tradition and Change*, London, 1919.
Westminster Review, July, 1881.
Wieten, Dr. A. A. S. *Mrs. Radcliffe*, Her Relation towards Romanticism, Amst. Diss., 1926.
Williams, Harold. *Modern English Writers*, London, 1918.
Zimmern, H. *Maria Edgeworth*, Eminent Women Series, London, 1883.